Prayers to She Who Is

GOD OUR MOTHER

Jean Morningstar, snjm '94

Prayers to She Who Is

WILLIAM CLEARY

WITH DRAWINGS BY

Jean Morningstar, SNJM

· · ·

FOREWORD BY

Joan Chittister, OSB

CROSSROAD | NEW YORK

1995
The Crossroad Publishing Company
370 Lexington Avenue, New York, NY 10017

Library of Congress Cataloging-in-Publication Data

Cleary, William.
    Prayers to She who is / William Cleary : with drawings by Jean
Morningstar : Foreword by Joan Chittister.
        p.   cm.
    Includes bibliographical references.
    ISBN 0-8245-1527-7 (pb)
    1. Femininity of God—Prayer-books and devotions—English.
2. Prayers. I. Johnson, Elizabeth A., 1941– She who is.
II. Title.
BT153.M6C44   1995
242'.8—dc20   95-37795
                                                                    CIP

In memoriam
Margaret Graham Bartlett
(1897–1972)
who taught all her children
what unconditional love is
and
Ella Theresa Merritt
(1874–1962)
who taught us freedom by
trying everything once
women who blessed me by being
like God
a mother and a grandmother

Contents

Foreword

BY JOAN CHITTISTER

*I*t didn't happen in one step. At least four separate incidents brought me to this point.

The first one occurred in the late '60's but I haven't gotten over it yet. The night their mother died, I was one of the people who undertook to get her six-year-old twins ready for bed. As each child ran down the hall fresh from his bath, he was rubbed down, bundled into pajamas, and held a little. For the adults in the house it was a sad and empty night. For the children it was a time for thinking, for explaining, for understanding why and where and how things were now. Jimmy, the first twin out of the tub, was sitting on my knee waiting for his brother. "Well," he said, fresh from first grade catechism class and looking up pensively at the crucifix, "by this time Momma's in God's stomach." I felt my religious sensibilities lurch a little. "No, no, Jimmy," I corrected him, "not God's stomach, God's arms. Momma is in God's arms now," I taught clearly and firmly. "God's arms?" Jimmy repeated, surprised and even a little chagrined, I thought. "Of course, Jimmy," I went on, repeating the old images, reinforcing half a consciousness of the nature of God. Then, finally, moved by his incredulity and fascinated enough to listen for a change, I couldn't stand it any more and asked with curiosity, if not with humility, "Jimmy, why ever would you think that mommy is in God's stomach?" "Well," the little boy answered with great certainty and patient logic. "Sister says that God is all around us. And God's stomach is the only place that I can think where you can be if God is all around you." At that moment I began to understand the womb of God. It affected me that night and it affects me even more now.

As the years went by, Jimmy finally got educated beyond pristine reason. Schooled and shaped and restricted by years of narrower images of God, he took on the masculine names for God—King, Lord, Father—and became quite orthodox, quite limited in his thinking about creation, about the Divine, just like the rest of us, I'm sure. I, on the other hand, was never able to forget his less patriarchal, far more theological revelation to me about the nature of God. It was a six-year-old who first taught me to think of She Who Is.

In the second instance, I found myself doing graduate work in Communication Theory at the very moment in academic history when philosophers, semanticists, and psychologists began to agree that thought does not shape language, language shapes thought. The words I use, in other words, determine the thoughts I think— about myself, about the world, about life and all its relationships, including my relationship with God and God's relationship with me, with us. The thought began to burrow into my soul like grass cracking cement. Who was this male God, I thought, who created women but wanted nothing to do with them, except of course at a subservient distance? Six-year-olds, I began to discover are danger-ously close in mentality to university professors. Or vice versa, perhaps.

Finally, at Call to Action, the great assembly of the Church held in Detroit in 1976 as part of the plethora of activities scheduled to coincide with the bicentennial celebration of the United States, I was on the quiet, unnoticed, pathetically small seven-person sub-committee on language that emerged out of the section of "Women in Church and Society." The other two hundred or so delegates in that particular conference segment concentrated on far weightier matters. They wanted church commissions on the status of women, the theological justification for the ordination of women, the social equality of women, the political involvement of women at the high-est of organization levels. No one paid much attention to the idea of language as an item of major importance to the issue. No one paid much attention to us at all. I predicted to the small group dedicated to the subject of language in liturgy, in fact, that every other recommendation but ours would pass without protest in the General assembly but that ours on inclusive language would be a struggle all the way. The committee laughed a little at the thought. Who could possibly agree to the ordination of women and question the use of two pronouns for the human race and the emphasis on the purely spiritually nature of God, as distinct from the anthropomorphic notion of a male God in a patriarchal church? The laughing did not last very long. Clearly, the Christian community, entrenched in a bad biology that had been theologized by the church, knew intuitively that the real revolution started with pronouns, not with proposals for ordination.

This reluctance to broaden, change, complete the image of God by moving beyond fatherhood—as if "fatherhood" were the sole element of creation, as if semen were the only raw material of the human race and women merely its incubators—left the human psyche deeply scarred and theology in contradiction with itself. What we taught we did not demonstrate. What we believed we did not accept. Patriarchy—the domination, oppression, ownership, and control by the fathers—became the Divine Order of the day and with it the rape of the earth and the rape of the women, as well. Then Jimmy and graduate school and an assembly locked in mortal combat over the name of the God whose name is "I am" began to come together for me in a torrent of pain, a rush of awareness, and an immeasurable depth of disillusionment with a church that called itself "True."

The fact is that nothing will really change until we change the language, until we learn to think differently, until we learn to see women as an equal image of God and the images of God as birthing mother, loving spirit, passionate compassion, heart of justice, and womb of the universe.

No, a person does not come to this point from one point only. At least I did not. Experience, a developed sense of selfness, and theology all lead the way. But language, we must never fail to remember, either reveals the revelation—or obscures it.

These prayers embody in their language a fuller picture of the God who birthed us. Because of them the world is now a softer, safer place, and God is a God big enough to be worthy of adoration.

The very act of praying them is Good News for women, Good News for the universe, Good News for the Church.

Joan D. Chittister

A Note from the Artist

JEAN MORNINGSTAR, SNJM

For many years, God, who is an incomprehensible mystery, has been presented in the Church as male. We know, in reality, that this cannot be true since God has no gender, but most people have accepted all three persons of the Trinity as exclusively masculine.

Jesus uses all sorts of images to teach us something about God. One of them is God as a father. What has not been emphasized is that he also compares God to light, to a woman searching for a lost coin, to a shepherd, and to a bakerwoman. Scripture is replete with other images of the Divine: a rock, a wind, a woman giving birth, a pillar of fire, wisdom, a mother bird, and a midwife.

To focus exclusively on God in the image of father or as masculine is to limit our experience of God. It is much richer and more truthful also to consider God as feminine. Using female images to refer to the Divine Mystery, however, seems to evoke negative reactions in many people. It is not upsetting or illogical to them to compare God to a rock or fire, but using feminine images or to refer to God as "she" seems to them to be an insult to our God. Undoubtedly, centuries of male domination and degradation of women have contributed to this negative attitude.

The illustrations that are presented in this publication are all feminine. Since a male God has been overemphasized for centuries, it is my hope that considering God in other ways will open up new and rich perspectives of the Divine Mystery.

Ten years ago, I studied with Matthew Fox, who introduced to me the idea that God could be considered in feminine as well as masculine terms. This concept radically changed my ideas about

God and my relationship with her. Recently, I read Elizabeth Johnson's book, *She Who Is*. Both of these experiences inspired me to draw these feminine images of God, and I gratefully dedicate this work to them.

Jean Morningstar, SNJM

Preface

*I*f you have opened this book to this page, I assume you care about prayer.

Question: does theology help prayer?

If you think it does, the following pages may interest you. Every one of these one hundred and twelve prayers is anchored in the revolutionary theology of Elizabeth Johnson, whose 1992 book *She Who Is* won the coveted Louisville Grawemeyer award for 1993 and made publishing history for a book of its kind. I believe *She Who Is* to be a foundational book for rebuilding Christianity from the ground up: a permanent "scripture" in this new moment in religious history, new because of the gradual arrival of strong new images and names for God: She Who Is, for instance.

But how is theology helpful for prayer? L. T. Johnson said in a *Commonweal* review that the book *She Who Is* provided "a vision of God worthy of prayer" and that the author gave him a newfound "freedom to pray."

That review was the inspiration for *Prayers to She Who Is*.

Theology helps prayer, I believe, by expanding both vision and freedom, though the vision is largely darkness and the freedom can be frightening. Test the prayers for those qualities.

Though this book has a progress of its own, the order of the prayers is essentially arbitrary and mural-like, an open-it-anywhere prayerbook—but not the kind of prayers that are uttered in response to life events or in celebration of the liturgical season.

Instead, these might be called "pondering prayers," or "theological prayers," their words often taken directly from the closely reasoned pages of *She Who Is*: "a God of Mystery" becomes "You,

God of Mystery." Those already familiar with *She Who Is* will recognize the thought and often even the words of Johnson. Others may be led to their own reading of the original work *She Who Is*.

Hopefully, all will recognize something unique about these prayers, due, in large part, to the extraordinary originality of Johnson's thought, and the level of poetic inspiration she achieves. If what results seems diffuse at first, the hope is that the richness of theology will not only deepen one's experience of the divine, but will enable readers to name the incomprehensible Mystery more accurately.

William Cleary
Shelburne, Vermont

· I ·

. . . the mystery that surrounds human lives . . .

What is the right way to speak to God? This is a question of unsurpassed importance, for speech to and about **the mystery that surrounds human lives** and the universe itself is a key activity of a community of faith. In that speech the symbol of God functions as the primary symbol of the whole religious system, the ultimate point of reference for understanding experience, life, and the world. Hence the way in which a faith community shapes language about God implicitly represents what it takes to be the highest good, the profoundest truth, the most appealing beauty. Such speaking, in turn, powerfully molds the corporate identity of the community and directs its praxis. . . .

Elizabeth A. Johnson, *She Who Is,* p. 4

1 *

WHEN I THINK OF YOU
when renewing a spiritual search

When I think of you, Holy Mystery, as She Who Is,
    I know instantly that you are turned toward me,
    for the female persons I know
    are consistently gifted with relatedness.[1]
I also know instantly you are the kind of God
    who would never ignore
    even the most insignificant, powerless child of your womb,
    and who burns with fury over the abuse of any that are yours.
When I think of you as She Who Is,
    I feel your motherly exuberance and vitality
    passing from you to me,
    and the force of your patient loving-kindness
    in urging my best self into action.
You are the God "in whom we live and move and have our
      being."
By that I implicitly name you Creator Mother and She Who Is
    since mothers are the only beings we know
    in whom others live and move and have their being.[2]
Although I know almost nothing about you except that you must
      exist
    and be reflected in your creatures,
    each day I launch into the search for you full of expectations,
    knowing instinctively that my quest
    pleases you immensely.

Creator Mystery, birthing, guiding, freeing,
In you we live and move and have our being.

2 *

MOTHER OF THE UNIVERSE
when rejoicing in existence

Holy Creator, mother of the universe,
    unoriginate, living source of all that exists,
    it is you who generates the life of all creatures
    since you yourself, in the beginning and continuously,
    supply the power of being within all being.
Mother-like, you freely chose to give life to all creatures
    without calculating a return,
    loving us inclusively,
    delighting in our clownish ways,
    joyfully uttering the basic affirmation:
    It is good that you exist. . . .[3]
It is music to our ears.
We rejoice continually in your affirmation and hear it in our
    hearts.

Creator Mother, singing, caring, freeing,
In you we live and move and have our being.

3 *

NAMING TOWARD GOD
thinking rightly about Holy Mystery

Nameless God, God Beyond Naming—
    no, we cannot accurately name you
    but we can "name toward you."[4]
We can see enough into the darkness of your mystery to know
      this:
    what you have made carries your fingerprints.
We discover magnificent order and intelligibility in what you have
      made
    so we can give you the name "Divine Intelligence."
Adding the belief that you are a good and generous God,
    we can stretch to the name "Holy Wisdom."
    It is not your name, but it points toward you,
      names toward you.
That name, Wisdom, or Sophia (in Greek), a favorite in our
      Scriptures,
    is arguably an older religious tradition
    than is the patriarchal name Father which we give you so
      often.[5]
So we call upon you;
    Wisdom, Holy Creator; hear our prayer.
    Divine Intelligence, Holy Creator; you are our guide.
    Goodness Infinite, Holy Creator; we reverence you.

Sophia, She Who Is, inspiring freeing,
In you we live and move and have our being.

4 *

WORLD OF WOMEN
searching for words for God

God-Mystery around us and within us,
    Boundless Energy and Passion and Unimaginable Wisdom,
    we honor your presence each time we break the bonds of
        language
      to speak toward you.
Deep in our bones most of us, alas, "know" you as a masculine
      being:
    "the Lord," "Heavenly Father."
    That feels correct since almost everything around us implies
      that men—
      for instance, lords or fathers—
    are superior to women;
      our families, our industries,
      our governments, our entertainments, our churches usually
        presume as much.
When we come to attend to the world of women,
    the unexpected scope of their ways of knowing,
    their striking gift for relationship and rootedness,
    their physical carrying of all new human life
      and their courage in giving it birth in awesome pain,
    their intelligence, good judgment, vitality, beauty, and
      longevity—
    when we attend to this, we quickly see
      that the world of women
      reflects a long-neglected aspect of your own "inclusive"
        mystery,
    so that in naming toward you
    we can no longer neglect those names that suggest
    all the intimacy and giftedness of female persons:
    Mother, Sister, Beloved Friend, Grandmother, Intimate Other.
We prefer such names for you at times
    because they imply a kind of divine caring that goes out,
      as women so often do,
      to the outcast, the hopeless cases,

the most despised, the most vulnerable,
as well as the kind of fierceness in anger and outrage
we see in the Mothers of the Disappeared,
the biblical mother bear separated from her cubs,
and the protectiveness over children
which mothers everywhere are justifiably renowned for.[6]
Creator Mother-Sophia, Holy Wisdom,
you bless us this day.
We cherish your caringness for us,
and thank you for giving us birth.

*Creator Mother, birthing, guiding, freeing,
In you we live and move and have our being.*

5 ✳

GIVER OF LIFE
when feeling awed by life

You, Mother God, are the giver of life and the lover of life,
  pervading the cosmos and all of its inter-related creatures with
    life.
If you were to withdraw your divine presence,
  everything—ourselves, our world, our history, our future—
  would go back to nothing.
We thank you for life, Holy God,
  and we ask for an ever-growing love of life
  and a heart of gratitude and liveliness.[7]
Gift us with that caringness that extends
  to all life, with reverence and energy,
  to the health and healing of our precious planet earth
  and all her life forms.

Living Mystery, leading, loving, freeing,
In you we live and move and have our being.

6 *

A WILDNESS

experiencing amazement

There is a wildness in your Divine Mystery, my God,
  a seeming randomness in the beauty of this world
  as well as in every frightening disaster,
  an oddness and awesome violence in the process of evolution,
  an originality in creation—that outflanks all our expectations.
We would tame you, Free and Holy One, and domesticate you
  but the effort fails.
The world you've put us into is inexhaustibly awesome and
    surprising,
    and it speaks of creative forces ever more unknown and not
      intelligible to us.
Wild, Fascinating Artist-Creator of Everything,
  guide our hearts and heads as we speak of you and to you:
  we know not who you are,
    where you are, how you can be what—and whatever—you
      are.
Rather than seek to break our idols from the past,
  give us ever more meaningful bridges of imagination.
True, we will never know you clearly in idols or icons
  but we seem to have no other path:
  our minds reach out in images,
  seeing your "words" everywhere,
  spoken in what you have created.
Guide our hearts, Holy Mystery, that they may not be overly
    grave
  or compulsively serious.
We would harmonize with your own freedom and randomness,
  trusting our future to your perfect care.
You are our God.[8]

Free Creative Wisdom, guiding, freeing,
In you we live and move and have our being.

7 ✳

MORE THAN BEING
when thankful for faith's vision

Surrounding-Me Mystery, Within-living Spirit Creator,
   you are more than Being:
   you are Vitality, Wisdom, Caring,
   Inexhaustible Inventiveness, Superabundance of Actuality,
   Ocean of Mystery, of Joy and Compassion,
   Inexhaustible Furnace of Energy,
   burning with longing for justice in this world you have made,
   bursting with creativity and delight,
   bearing all the world's pain with infinite compassion.
I give thanks for your inconceivable strength
   that gives life to the world, radiance to the cosmos, and hope
     to the future.[9]

Creator Spirit, loving, guiding, freeing,
In you we live and move and have our being.

8 *

WE POINT ONLY
finding our way toward the mystery

Our essentially incomprehensible God,
  of what use are our words *about* you,
  or words—like these
    directed to you?
  In almost every sense you are absolute mystery.
  But at least we can say this:
    our words point, point toward you.
We wonder: are you not divinely "good"?
  Yes, but not in the way creatures are good,
    not in the way we know created goodness
    for we can't imagine goodness without limits.[10]
Has "goodness" lost all meaning then? No, it points.
  The word goodness points toward you
  and guides us in our faith and our prayer:
  you are truly but incomprehensibly good.
We know your goodness, each of us in our own way,
  but cannot grasp it, comprehend it, predict it, or define it.
You are good, and you are goodness:
  this we infer despite your seeming absence.
We look to you in love—for we always love goodness:
  we look, but we see mostly darkness,
    your incomprehensible otherness,
    your being beyond all being we know.
Holy Goodness, incomprehensible but very near,
  you have our wordless adoration
  though we may no longer bow or kneel to you
    as we might to an earthly patriarch.
  Instead we look to you in confidence and trust,
    unafraid to show you our face and all that we are.
  You are our love and the object of all our heart's longings.
May not only our names,
  but our whole being this moment point to you.

Holy She Who Is, accepting, freeing,
In you we live and move and have our being.

9 ✳

NEW REVELATION

when appreciating the strength of women

Holy Mystery, the human search for you
    moves ahead all over the earth
    every day, and every hour.
In this search, there are moments of particular success,
    rare times when an individual or a group come to know you
    on a new level altogether.
Such a moment, we believe, is occurring
    now that the human community awakens at last
        to a new valuation of women
    and as women themselves awaken to their own human worth.
It is a new event in the religious history of humankind,
    a kind of new revelation,[11]
    and a revolution in the concept of the divine,
    built now on the gradual world-spreading discovery of women
        as fully equal to men,
    made, like them, in the image of God.[12]
Be with us, Holy Mystery, and give us a bright dawning of
    understanding.
If we have been blinded somehow in perceiving this new
    revelation,
    open the eyes of our hearts now to take it in fully
    and to recognize at last the full possibilities
        of this analogical knowledge that is also an "unknowing,"
    and the comfort we may have in a new sense
        of your incomprehensible mystery.

Creating God, enlightening and freeing,
In you we live and move and have our being.

10 *

THERE CAN BE HOPE
toward a positive spirituality

Holy God beyond all human thought,
    in faith we offer ourselves to your mystery.
   You are the one about whose essence we know very little
    except that it is to exist.
What you are is existence without cause or limit,
   the birthing mother and inventor of all we have ever known,
   yet beyond it all to an infinite degree—
  which carries us into the deepest darkness
    that is also a kind of unknowing.
  Yet in this unknowing knowledge, we do know something
     crucial
    to our own survival as humane members of our race:
    that there can be optimism, hope,
      and a legitimate search for meaning in the world,
    for if you are the one whose essence is your existence,
     a necessarily compassionate existence it must be,
    judging from the strengths of the persons you have made
     in your own image.
Your being is necessary and infinite and eternal
  and moreover compassionate and therefore relational,
  with all the implications that relationality brings:
   you are not isolated or unconcerned or distant from any of us
   but care infinitely for us, each and all.[13]

Compassionate Mystery, loving, drawing, freeing,
In you we live and move and have our being.

· II ·

. . . *the female figure of Wisdom* . . .

The most extended biblical instance of female
imagery of the Spirit occurs in the wisdom
literature where the Spirit's functions are depicted
as acts of Woman Wisdom. **The female figure of
Wisdom** is the most acutely developed
personification of God's presence and activity in
the Hebrew scriptures. Not only is the
grammatical gender of the word for wisdom
feminine (*hokmah* in Hebrew, *sophia* in Greek),
but the biblical portrait of Wisdom is
consistently female, casting her as sister, mother,
female beloved, chef and hostess, teacher,
preacher, maker of justice and a host of other
women's roles. In every instance Wisdom
symbolizes transcendent power pervading and
ordering the world, both nature and human
beings, interacting with them all to lure them
onto the path of life. . . .

Elizabeth A. Johnson, *Women, Earth
and Creator Spirit*, p. 52

Song of the Universe

11 *

FAITHFUL SOPHIA
when calling God Sophia

Who are you, Faithful Sophia whom we meet in Scripture?
  Are you not a fascinating female personification of the divine
      mystery?
Holy Mystery, beyond naming or understanding,
  whom our forebears, in profoundest awe,
  gave an unpronounceable name—YHWH—
  sometimes we shall call upon you as "Sophia,"
  the scriptural name meaning Wisdom.[14]
We find you in the Book of Wisdom:
  You fashion all that exists
      and pervade it with your pure and people-loving spirit,
  You are all-knowing, all-powerful, and present everywhere,
      renewing all things.
  Active in creation, you also work in history to save your chosen
      people,
      guiding and protecting us
      through the vicissitudes of liberating struggle.
  You send your servants to proclaim your invitation to
      communion.
  By your light kings govern justly
      and the unjust meet their punishment."
All such ancient Scriptural descriptions
  help us to grope about in your mystery,
  searching for you, our elusive parenting divinity.
Are you there?
Is it you, Sophia God, our God?

Sophia, She Who Is, empowering, freeing,
In you we live and move and have our being.

12 *

WOMEN MIRRORING GOD
for love of She Who Is

Creator Mystery,
   since all humans are made in your image,
   the distinctive gifts of women,
     quite apart from any life-bearing function,
   mirror your being:
     an instinct for an ethic based on caring,
     an intelligence that favors the un-abstract
       and the connectedness of all things,
     a unique sympathy for those in pain
     and a distinct ability for human connection and relationship.
All this images your divine mystery and fills the world with
     hope.[15]
Aware of this as we are,
   can you help us deal with religious leaders who name you
     with exclusively male names,
   implying thereby the inadequacy of women's reality
     to represent the divine?
Give us a little of your patience—and enlightened impatience,
   your tolerance of our dim vision and illusion-prone minds
   along with your fierce drive toward a more just and
     enlightened society.

Sophia, She Who Is, empowering, freeing,
In you we live and move and have our being.

13 *

O God of many names:
    our "Father" whom we have addressed all our lives
      in the words Jesus taught us,
    our "Life-giver" and "Mother"
      whom we now address in the words that theologians give us:
    "the One Who Is"—as Moses taught us—
      with us before we knew you, feeding us, caring,
        protecting, supporting us,
        healing our wounds,
        understanding when few others understood.
There is a kind of threeness in our experience of you:[15]
    first as Life-giving Spirit and creative spark within all creation,
      invisible and free as the wind,
      awesomely present in all that is mysterious, powerful, and
        promising;
    then as Companion of our lives,
      wise Divine Wisdom around us and within us and in our
        sacred writers,
      an Infinite Caring Intelligence,
        who even becomes incarnate in Jesus
        and in all who, like Jesus, do messianic deeds;
    finally as Source of all that is,
      Parent of all of us born of your love,
      our Mother/Father,
      Creator, Home-Builder, Teacher,
      Accompanier, Guide, and end of all that is.
O God,
    your creating this world so inter-related in multiple ways
    suggests to us a multiple inter-related dynamism, a
      communion,
      within your own Holy Mystery:
      a Holy Communion and Communioning
    —of Love, Wisdom, and Creative Energies.
Holy Spirit, Word, Source!

Everything turns us toward you!
You are our Origination, our Enlightenment, and our Advocate,
   Incomprehensible Livingness, Wisdom, and Caring.
We bless you as best we can:
   the thought of you, the reality of you, the presence of you:
the One Who Is, our God.

Gracious Mystery God, creating, freeing,
In you we live and move and have our being.

14 *

WORLD CHANGE
opening new doors in prayer

Holy Mystery, I know just calling you "mother"
    instead of only "father"
is much more than a word change.
It is a world change.[17]
Calling you *She Who Is* instead of *He Who Is*
    changes everything.
Whatever name or symbol we use for you "functions"
    and puts everything we have known in a new light,
    rearranges all our world's furniture
    and spins new imaginings in our minds.
Help us discard the limitations of our inherited God-talk
    so that we can look at you with a new innocence,
Awesome, Amazing, Bewildering Divinity,
    Source of us all.
Guide us in our search for you.

Sophia, She Who Is, inspiring, freeing,
In you we live and move and have our being.

15 *

INADEQUATE NAMES

considering names new and old

God-Companion, Creator-who-is,
you burst through the masks of our old male patriarchal god
   of so many inadequate names—
   which rather name our foolish childishness than name you:
   "Lord," "Father," "King," "Lord Omnipotent."
Though we no longer are content with these broken masks of the
      past,
   at least we know that masks will no longer misguide us.[18]
They were once helpful light in the deepest darkness
   but now they obscure your being
   which in fact is better expressed by quite opposite concepts:
   a servant God, a fellow-victim who chooses no defense,
   a co-sufferer of political whim, Being most vulnerable.
Creator of freedom, enduring the costs of a generosity beyond all
      imagining,
   we thank you for your immediacy, for your nearness,
   for your creating caringness, for the mystery of your
      vulnerability.

Caring Mystery, loving, guiding, freeing,
In you we live and move and have our being.

16 *

HILDEGAARD'S VISION
following the guidance of the mystics

This day, how shall we name you
  or name-toward-you,
Holy Mystery?
Are you not, as Hildegaard of Bingen put it,
  the life of our life,
  the life of all creatures,
  the very connectedness between all creatures,
  a burning fire who sparks, ignites, inflames, and kindles hearts,
  a guide through the mist,
  a balm for wounds,
  a shining serenity,
  an overflowing fountain that spreads refreshment on all sides?
Holy God, are you not life itself,
  movement, color, radiance,
    and restorative stillness in the din?
Is it not your power that re-kindles the greening of springtime
    in nature and in our souls?
Is it not you who purify, absolve,
  strengthen, heal,
  and gather the perplexed, and seek the lost?
You pour the comforting balm of contrition
    into hardened hearts.
It is you, Spirit-Sophia, who play music in the soul,
  you who awaken mighty hopes around the world,
  blowing like the wind everywhere.[19]
We give thanks for your glory and your goodness.

Spirit, She Who Is, inspiring, freeing,
In you we live and move and have our being.

17 *

NAMELESS ONE
reaching out toward Mystery

We look to you, Mysterious God,
   a presence of divine Wisdom
     standing under and within all creation,
     as though you were a "Mother Nature,"
     caring for everything,
     holding everything in life and in being,
   a secret loving presence
   who cares passionately for us in a private and hidden way,
     invisible but vigorously living and always near.
In all metaphorical names for you, Sophia, Eternal Wisdom,
   we admit there is infinitely less light than there is darkness,
   less similarity than there is otherness.
What little we know of you is dwarfed
   by your endless Unknowability.[20]
We may see your strength at work in our little world,
   but there are near infinite stretches of space
   (we can point to them but not see them)
   where you create and sustain and guide a creation
   wholly unknown to us and utterly beyond our imagining.
Sophia-Spirit, we stammer in your presence.
See our wordless face, looking to you.
We are yours.

Nameless God, creating, leading, freeing,
In you we live and move and have our being.

18 *

DEEPER DARKNESS
admitting bewilderment

The revelation of your existence, Holy God,
   is not an enlightenment, pure and simple,
   but really a deepening of the darkness:
for if you cannot <u>not</u> exist,
   you also, it seems, can not simply exist
     in the divine sovereignty we have long assigned to you,
   conditions in our world being what they are.
Are atheists not seeing
   one aspect of the mystery we may be missing?
Often we must admit to an impression of a divine absence,[21]
   a seeming vacuum of wisdom in what exists,
   a lack of divine direction in history,
   an inexplicable hiddenness of divine compassion
     for the outcast, the helpless, and the poor.
It is almost unthinkable
   that you could bring this world into being,
   and yet know everything that is, and all that might happen—
considering the almost unrelieved horrors
    that occur every day:
   the defeats of compassion and even of civility,
   the triumphs of greed,
   the ghastly twists that illness gives to vulnerable human
      natures,
   the almost diabolical advance of disease and accidental injury—
    to even the most innocent:
   in short, the destruction
   of so much promise and forward momentum.
Do you exist beneath and within all this, Holy God?
Are you She Who Is, our Creator Mother,
   existing in infinite caringness and strength within it all?
What darkness there is around, beneath, even within the light!

Holy Mystery, loving, leading, freeing,
In you we live and move and have our being.

23

19 *

ALL ARE GIFTS
knowing great gratitude

Holy Spirit-Sophia and Breath of life,
    named Ruah in our Hebrew scriptures,
  all the gifts that build the life of the community
  we credit to your inspiring, resting upon
  or moving within different persons:
      the courage and wisdom of inspiring leaders,
      the strength of fearless liberators, the energy of prophets and
          seers,
      the wisdom of philosophers and teachers,
      the creativity of musicians, poets, dancers, and artists,
      are all direct gifts of your spirit.
Above all, prophecy, with its strong ethical dimension,
  is a sign of special endowment by your power.[22]
We accept this especially in your prophet Jesus
  who so uniquely incarnated your wisdom.
It is you who creates the covenantal bonds
  that make of Israel, and subsequently of all the nations,
  the people of God.
We would be your people, Sophia Wisdom,
  your nation, your flock,
  great shepherd of being, She Who Is.

Ruah, Breath of Life, inspiring, freeing,
In you we live and move and have our being.

20 *
LOVING THE ONLY GOD
feeling God near

Whoever loves and worships you, Holy Sophia,
  is loving the one and only God
    but a God who can be given personifications of different kinds,
      as the human imagination tries to cope
      with your unimaginable being and creative actions.[23]
We give you our humble worship, Sophia-God,
  knowing your loving presence is closer to us than we are to
      ourselves,
  and deeper in all the details of our lives than we can imagine.
You are a profound comfort to us in our darkness,
  for to live in a world created by Wisdom
  can quell temptations to despair and discouragement
    when we feel surrounded by what is chaotic, absurd, and
      unjust.
You, Rescuing Presence, eager to help us,
  who appeared in the Burning Bush
  with compassion for an enslaved people,
  are with us through all our sorrows,
  as we reach out to harmonize
  with your all-wise creativity and intelligence,
    vast energies, and unlimited caringness.

God of Life, empowering and freeing,
In you we live and move and have our being.

· III ·

. . . consulting human experience . . .

Consulting human experience is an identifying mark of virtually all contemporary theology, as indeed has been the case at least implicitly with most of the major articulations in the history of Christian theology. Listening to the questions and struggles of the people of an era, their value systems, and deepest hopes, gives theology of the most diverse kinds an indispensable clue for shaping inquiry, drawing the hermeneutical circle, revising received interpretations, and arriving at new theological insight. Feminist reflection is therefore not alone in its use of human experience as a resource for doing theology. What is distinctive, however, is its specific identification of the lived experience of women, long derided or neglected in androcentric tradition, as an essential element in the theological task. . . .

Elizabeth A. Johnson, *She Who Is,* p. 61

21 *

WOMEN'S EXPERIENCE
expanding the concept of God

Sophia-God,
   just as we have learned much about your divinity
      from men's experience
      (since men are made in your image),
   and similarly, from women's experience
      (since women also are made in your image),
      we add the knowledge that your love always includes
         a ready openness to the ones loved,
         a vulnerability to their experience,
         a solidarity with their well-being,
         and necessarily joy in their joys and grief with their
            sorrows.
It is your love for us of this latter kind, Holy Mystery,
   that not only suggests suffering of some kind in you
   but also guarantees your pleasure
      in all that is beautiful, harmonious,
      promising, and creative in us and our world.[24]
Holy Creator, how unimaginable is your solidarity
   with our every experience, how crucial your presence to it all.

Caring God, compassionate and freeing,
In you we live and move and have our being.

22 *

speaking to the God of action

Holy Mystery, She/He Who Is,
   we most properly think of you
   as a verb, an action, an activity,
   not a noun or a "thing."[25]
You are Being, Loving, Knowing, Creating:
   an inner-communioning of creativity, energy, and wisdom,
   an empowering Presence.
Lighten our hearts with a liveliness
   in rhythm with your own vibrant activity.
Enlighten us with your fascinating, incomprehensible mystery.

Vibrant Mystery, present, guiding, freeing,
In you we live and move and have our being.

23 *

when turning to God in hope

Holy Wise Divine Communion,
   you are more than the ground of our being:
   you are the ground of what should be
     and what we trust will be.[26]
You are the ground of justice and of hope.
Is it not true that as we grow close to you,
we will grow close
     to your passionate desires for justice and abundant life?
Holy Wisdom, Sophia, She Who Is,
   we pray we are not far from you.

Wise Empowering God, inspiring, freeing,
In you we live and move and have our being.

24 *

SHARING IN YOUR FIRE
honoring the Fire who speaks

Holy Fire of the Burning Bush,
    who spoke to our prophet Moses out of unquenchable fire,
    fiery caringness for everything you have made,
        agonizing with all who live in exile,
        and tortured by your compassion with our multiple
            enslavements,
        flaming unconsumed through thousands of years—
with Aquinas we observe your analogous mirroring
    of a fire igniting whatever it encounters:
        everything that exists does so
        by participation in the fire of your divine being.
Similarly everything that acts is energized by your divine act.[27]
Everything that brings something else into being
    does so by sharing in divine creative power.
We are yours.
Set our hearts on fire.
As you set the Sinai bush burning without its being consumed,
    so burn within whatever within us can be warmed
        and set immortally aglow by your presence.
Come, Burning Fire,
    covenanting with us for liberation:
    let us be the vehicles of your liberating and covenanting fire.

Fiery Mystery, loving, guiding, freeing,
In you we live and move and have our being.

25 *

the God who sets us free

Holy Voice of Burning Bush and Agonizing Compassion,
 you approach us in our Sacred Scripture
  as the ground of freedom itself,
  demonstrating your own freedom,
  inspiring in us a longing for freedom,
  and urging us to work
   for freedom and justice throughout our world
    community.[28]
Be ever in our minds and hearts
 so we too become authentic lovers of freedom and justice,
 insisting on our birthright as images of you.

Burning Mystery, caring, helping, freeing,
In you we live and move and have our being.

26 *

FIERY MYSTERY

when praying for freedom

You are mystery,
   God of Sinai and of the bush burning unconsumed,
      pouring out compassion, promising deliverance,
      stirring up a human sense of mission toward that end.[29]
Make us partners with you in your astonishing earthy project,
   the enlightenment of those who do not see,
   the liberation of all held captive by illusion,
   the full growth of the earth community in freedom and joy.

Caring Mystery, burning, leading, freeing,
In you we live and move and have our being.

27 *

PRESENT IN SCRIPTURE
facing the Mystery ever new

Dear God,
   as you are intimate to everything that lives and acts
   so you must especially inspire and guide those
      who write compellingly of your presence and voice.
Where have you appeared more convincingly
   than in the writings about your Sinai self?
There you speak
   of knowing experientially what people are suffering
   and offer to create a solidarity with and among us
   that can ultimately bring about change: justice and peace.[30]
Then in your prophets and poets
   down to Jesus and beyond
   you are with us in their sayings and acts and writings.
We find you in all the love of justice there,
      our loving God,
   and affirm your presence within ourselves,
   inspiring us with the same desires.

Fiery Mystery God, inspiring, freeing,
In you we live and move and have our being.

28 *

KNOWING SELF BEST
discovering the self who prays

Fathomless Mystery
    I know myself best in your presence.[31]
Who I am is—
    your creation,
    a reflection of your communioning mystery,
    a guest of your being and your story,
    an act of your world-fashioning creativity.
I know myself fully only in the light of your sourcing,
    only in the phenomenon of your wildness and
        incomprehensibility,
    in the beauty and liveliness in my world,
    in my history, and my possibilities.
Empower us—empower me—
    to the stature of my full self,
    beyond the fences of a limited cultural vision,
    beyond the safety of conventional defenses.
Empower me as you empowered the real saints of our times:
    mothers who do not despair
      through the abuses of domestic and sexist oppression,
    artists and storytellers who follow inspiration into
        unpredictable mysteries,
    loving sisters who cast their net of care
      far and wide and deep and without ceasing,
    clear-eyed prophets
      who, while rallying a human circle
        to be empowered for freedom and justice,
      utter their visionings in the midst of danger, threat, and
        ridicule.
In your presence I have a self full of possibility
    and a path uniquely my own.
Be with me in mind and memory
    so I may name myself accurately,
    and build my life communally and creatively.

Holy Spirit God, inspiring, freeing,
In you we live and move and have our being.

29 *

AT THE LIMITS
when reaching toward the mystery

In my relatedness to you, Mysterious Communioning Spirit-
 Sophia,
  I know my own autonomy ever more distinctly,
  yet feel my rootedness and connections as well.[32]
At the limits of my autonomy,
  where I run up against the canyon walls of egotism and
    individualism,
  I find myself turned toward you,
  my source, my rootedness, and my meaning.
At the limits of my connectedness,
  when I feel myself alone,
  I reach toward you, my creator, my life, and my home.
Be with me, my God, create in me a heart for connectedness.

Caring Mystery, linking, weaving, freeing,
In you we live and move and have our being.

30 *

feeling inspired by God

When we speak of you as friend, Holy Mystery,
    and in names implying your love for us,
    we also indicate an agenda for human life.
    These convictions have consequences:
        we are loved in order to love,
        gifted in order to gift,
        and befriended in order to turn to the world
        as sisters and brothers in redeeming, liberating friendship.[33]
Give us, Creative Spirit, some of the astonishing graciousness
    that brought this world into existence.

Creator Mystery, birthing, guiding, freeing,
In you we live and move and have our being.

31 *

UNORIGINATE RADIANCE
relishing the light

Holy Mystery without origin,
    without source,
    without beginning,
it is you who generate everything that is
    and seek its flourishing.
From your unoriginate bright radiance
    stream forth all the lesser lights
    and all energy for resistance against evil.[34]
Grant us always enough vision
    to enjoy your radiance and catch fire from your energies.

Wise Enlightening Mystery, loving, freeing,
In you we live and move and have our being.

· IV ·

. . . *the Being of God* . . .

A . . . position, variously known as dialectical
theism, neoclassical theism, or, more typically,
panentheism, offers another, more congenial
model. As defined in *The Oxford Dictionary of
the Christian Church*, panentheism is "The belief
that **the Being of God** includes and penetrates
the whole universe, so that every part of it exists
in Him, but (as against pantheism) that this Being
is more than, and is not exhausted by, the
universe." Here is a model of free, reciprocal
relation: God in the world and the world in God
while each remains radically distinct. The relation
is mutual while differences remain and are
respected. As with classical theism no proportion
between finite creatures and divine mystery is set
up, the disparity between them is absolute. But
the absolute difference between Creator and
creature is encircled by God who is all in all. . . .

Elizabeth A. Johnson, *She Who Is*, p. 231

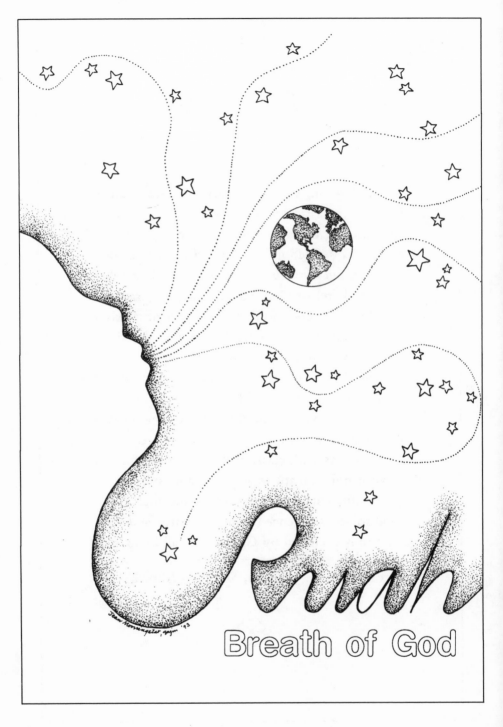

Breath of God

32 *

BOTH PRESENCES
facing the God beyond us

Holy Divine Mystery,
   in our search for you
   we discover you do not totally transcend us
     so as to be unreachable
   and do not totally inhabit us as to make us divine,
   but rather hold both presences in full strength,[35]
     our God and our All, our All and our God,
     our Creator, our Companion, and our homeward Guide!
We give thanks we are chosen
   to be part of this incomprehensible mystery.

Holy God, mysterious and freeing,
In you we live and move and have our being.

33 *

YO U E N C I R C L E U S
united forever with She Who Is

O God who is all in all,
    we have trouble imagining how we can exist
    in "panentheistic" relation to you:
    within you yet distinct from you.
Is it not like a tiny island encompassed by the boundless sea?
You encircle us in a way
    that generates in us a uniqueness, futurity, and self-
        transcendence,
    in a relation that sets us free
    and calls us to communal, personal, and cosmic shalom.[36]
All our powers of "resistance," ongoing fidelity, and renewal
    exist because of the power of your relationship to us
    that is stronger than death.
Even in death, you can never be other than present with us,
    your unforgettable children and companions in being.
    We are grateful.

Wise Encircling Mystery, loving, freeing,
In you we live and move and have our being.

34 *

A MUTUAL COINHERENCE
when enjoying God's presence

Holy God, existing everywhere and yet beyond all existences,
    we rejoice in a mutual coinherence with you
      whereby we exist within you, and you exist within us,
    and you are present throughout the universe
    with your inclusive caring and compassionate love.
Be with us and within us at this moment and forever.[37]

God within us all, empowering, freeing,
In you we live and move and have our being.

35 *

CONTINUOUSLY PRESENT
speaking to the God Who Is

Holy Creating Wisdom,
   your very being is relational
   and dwells not in isolation from the world
   but in reciprocal relation,
   sustaining its life,
   continuously resisting destructive powers of nonbeing.
You are active wherever there is a self-respecting love of freedom
    and a yearning for justice,
   approaching us from the future to attract us toward shalom.[38]
Be with us in our minds, in our hearts, and in our relationships.
Holy One Who Is, She/He Who Is, you are our God.

God of life and knowledge, guiding, freeing,
In you we live and move and have our being.

36 ✳

YOU WE AFFIRM
declaring God's presence in everything

It is you we affirm, Holy Mystery,
   in all the vitality, radical energy,
   originality, spontaneity, and charm
   we encounter in the very being-there of created existence,[39]
      of each particular lovely face,
      of each sunset display of originality,
      of each empowerment of human virtue and virtuosity.
You are the unoriginate welling-up of the fullness of life
   in which the whole universe participates.
We encounter you again and again and again
   and know that an eternity of such encounters
   will not begin to exhaust your endless mystery.

God of Beauty, loving, leading, freeing,
In you we live and move and have our being.

37 *

when viewing creation

In speaking of your deeds, Holy Mystery,
    we are pointing to the gracious, fascinating mystery of your
        divinity
    creating, indwelling, sustaining,
    resisting, recreating, challenging,
    guiding, liberating, and completing—
and all these are aspects of the single and unified engagement
    you have with the world.[40]
Behold us here in your presence,
    amazed at your wonderful deeds.

God within us all, empowering, freeing,
In you we live and move and have our being.

38 *

ENERGY FOR CHANGE
when giving thanks

You, Holy Mystery, are the source
  of transforming energy among all creatures.
You initiate novelty, instigate change,
  transform what is dead into new bursts of life.
Fertility is intimately related to your recreative power,
  as is the attractiveness of sex.
It is you who are ultimately playful, fascinating,
  pure and wise, luring human beings into the depths of love.[41]
It is you who move us all toward creativity and joy in the
    struggle,
  toward healing and liberation.
We give thanks for calling us into your vitality and strength.

Holy Womb of All, empowering, freeing,
In you we live and move and have our being.

39 *

LOVING SOPHIA

conversing with Spirit-Sophia

Spirit-Sophia,
Divine Wisdom that our scriptural authors believed in
    and preserved in our holy writings,
  you are a female personification
    of the God we have known all along by other names,
    especially that most mysterious and unpronounceable name
    written as "YHWH,"
    a personification of a God
      in creative and saving involvement with the world.[42]
You fashion all that exists, Holy Wisdom,
  and pervade it with your pure, people-loving spirit.
You are all knowing,
    even all powerful after the manner of love's irresistible but
      vulnerable power,
  present everywhere, renewing all things second by second.
As you are active in creation,
    you also work in history to rescue your chosen people
    (and all of us are chosen),
    guiding and protecting us through the vicissitudes of liberating
      struggle.
Your powerful words bring us hope.
You send your prophets to proclaim your invitation to
    communion.
It is by your light that enlightened leaders govern
  and the unjust are discovered in their greed and egoism.
You are involved with each of us
  in our relationships of loving, seeking, and finding.
May you be an unforgettable omnipresent companion
  in all we dream and do.

Great-hearted God, forgiving, guiding, freeing,
In you we live and move and have our being.

40 *

when calling upon God

Great and Holy Spirit,
   Ruah, breath of God, who, according to the Genesis story,
   swept creatively over the original waters of chaos,
   producing earth and cosmos,
we know you are the one true God,
   named over the years in many other ways:
   Lord, Savior, King, Father, Yahweh, the One Who Is
   and less often named Wisdom, Sophia, Mother.
Still, that title, Holy Spirit, *Sancte Spiritus,*
   names-toward-you with special aptness,
   suggesting a blowing wind, a storm,
   a stream of air, breath in motion,
   something dynamically in movement
   and impossible to pin down,
   your Holy Livingness
   creating, sustaining, and guiding all things
   and unable to be confined.[43]
Moving Invisible *Spiritus,* we honor your name,
   we are in awe of your presence,
   we welcome you,
   we sense your presence within and between us all,
   your creative and freeing power let loose in the world
   moving where you will, as you will,
   beyond anyone's control,
   lifegiving as a fresh breeze,
   awe-inspiring as tornado and cyclone,
   invisible but known in your effects: Wind-like Spirit!
Come, inspire us with your energies!

Spirit-Mystery, urging, guiding, freeing,
In you we live and move and have our being.

41 *

MUSIC IN MY SOUL
honoring the God of music

Holy Spirit and Unpredictable Wind of Infinite Possibility,
    we hear a music in our souls and beings
    and a melody deep in everything
    and especially between persons: is it You?
Is it you who plays music in the soul
    making melodies of praise and joy?[44]
Are you yourself perhaps the antiphonal melody between loving
    persons?
Is it you who constantly awaken in us the mighty hope
    that deep within the chaotic-seeming reality around us
    there is Goodness, Promise, Love enough for each and all of us
    and a home at journey's end?
Your existence is almost too good to be true.
Without knowledge of you our world would be utterly different.
We are thankful that you are revealed to us, our incomprehensible
    God.

God of harmony, inspiring, freeing,
In you we live and move and have our being.

· V ·

. . . *Jesus, a genuine Spirit-phenomenon* . . .

Christian faith is grounded on the experience that
God who is Spirit at work in the tragic and
beautiful world to vivify and renew all creatures
through the gracious power of her indwelling,
liberating love, is present yet again through the
very particular history of one human being, Jesus
of Nazareth. The one who is divine love, gift,
and friend becomes manifest in time in a concrete
gestalt, the loving, gifting, and befriending first-
century Jewish carpenter turned prophet.
According to the witness of Scripture, **Jesus is a
genuine Spirit-phenomenon,** conceived,
inspired, sent, hovered over, guided, and risen
from the dead by her power. In its etymological
and historical context, the early Christian
confession that Jesus is the Christ means precisely
this, that he is the Messiah, the anointed one, the
one anointed by the Spirit. Through human
history the Spirit who pervades the universe
becomes concretely present in a small bit of it.
Sophia pitches her tent in the midst of the world;
the Shekinah dwells among the suffering people
in a new way. In a word, Jesus is Emmanuel,
God with us. . . .

Elizabeth A. Johnson, *She Who Is*, p. 150

42 *

WISDOM-SENT MESSIAH
naming God "Spirit"

Spirit-Sophia,
  with the cooperation of Mary and Joseph
  you guided the messianic Jesus of Nazareth through his early
     years,
    then led him into the desert for his trial by fasting and
     revelation;
  you inspired him to quote from Isaiah
    in his career-opening words in his hometown synagogue,
    anointing him to preach good news to the poor,
     to proclaim release to captives and recovering of sight to the
     blind,
    to set at liberty those who are oppressed.[45]
Infinite Wisdom,
  you inspire each of us to find our own messianic mission,
  to live out our part of the Cosmic Christ,
    searching our own hearts for the guidance you give us,
  finding evidence of your creative light
  in the events that made us who we are,
  and in the stories of those around us with meaningful lives:
    we await your coming to illuminate our darkness.
Come, Holy Spirit, Wisdom,
  fill the hearts of your faithful
  and enkindle within them the fire of your divine light.
Send forth the creative breath of your Spirit
  that we may be newly created.
Renew through your coming the face of the earth.

Spirit-Sophia, guiding, caring, freeing,
In you we live and move and have our being.

43 *

YOUR INCARNATION IN JESUS
remembering Messiah

Once we have come to know you, Holy Mystery,
    as the one who is divine love, generosity, and friend,
    it becomes possible to recognize your incarnation
    in the loving and befriending first-century Jewish carpenter
        turned prophet,
    Jesus of Nazareth.[46]
As your Spirit dwelt uniquely in him,
    may your Spirit come upon us as well
    to make us a part of his messianic mystery
    and sacraments of the world's salvation.

Spirit of Jesus, guiding, caring, freeing,
In you we live and move and have our being.

44 *

SOPHIA'S CHILD
thanking God for Jesus

Sophia, Holy Wisdom,
   your incarnation in Jesus, the Wisdom of God,
   and our sacramental remembrance of it
   connects your Holy Mystery in an ongoing way,
      to concrete embodiment, to the world,
      to suffering and delight,
      to compassion and liberation
         in a way that can never be broken.[47]
We love the Child that you have sent, Sophia!
Give us the grace to carry on his mission.

Wisdom-Sophia, caring, loving, freeing,
In you we live and move and have our being.

45 *

YOUR PROPHET JESUS
when remembering the Christ

Gracious God,
   who in your care for your world
   sent us the prophet Jesus of Nazareth
   and filled him, as an incarnation of yourself,
      with the fire of your friendship, your love, and your
         gratuitous self-gift,
   we give thanks for the work of his coming
   and for the meaning of his tragic death:
for he has truly died
   and is gone from the midst of history according to the flesh.[48]
But in raising him from the dead according to the Gospels,
   you affirm that you shall have the last word
      for this executed victim of political injustice—
   and that word is life.
Your Jesus in all his physical and spiritual historicity
   is raised into glory by your power.
While his life is now hidden in your glory,
   his presence is known
      wherever two or three gather, bread is broken, the hungry
        fed.
From his death a Cosmic Christ has risen
   that includes potentially all humanity,
   molded in his christic pattern,
   dedicated to the building of a new heaven and a new earth.

Spirit of Jesus, leading, gracing, freeing,
In you we live and move and have our being.

46 *

ALL ARE LINKED
when turning to God

Spirit Sophia, infinite ocean of sympathy for all who suffer,
    through the human links of solidarity
        which you forged by your Holy Wisdom incarnate on the
            cross
    and through a messianic spirituality inspired by your Spirit,
        all those who suffer are connected with divine life,
        the ultimate ground of hope.
Thus, Holy God, our historical world
    is interwoven with your eternal livingness.
As in joy, so in pain we may turn to you and trust in your
        response,
    praying that we may endure the difficulties of life
        in solidarity with all the deprived and oppressed in the
            world,
        in union with your Wisdom incarnate in Jesus on the cross,
    and in that darkest faith where you most intimately dwell.[49]

Spirit Wisdom, guiding, caring, freeing,
In you we live and move and have our being.

47 *

THE CROSS OF JESUS
finding hope in defeat

Spirit of Wisdom,
   as the cross of Jesus is a parable
      that enacts your participation in the suffering of the world;
   and as the victory of love, both human and divine,
      that spins new life out of this disaster
      is expressed in our belief in a risen Christ,
   we pray for faith.
We would be confident
   that the overwhelming evil in the crucifixion of Jesus
   does not have the last word.
We trust that the suffering accompanying his life
   is neither passive, useless, nor divinely ordained,
   but is linked to your ways, Holy Mystery,
      of forging justice and peace in an antagonistic world.[50]
We link ourselves to the parable of that cross,
   and pray for solidarity with the Cosmic Christ
   everywhere struggling for justice and liberation in the world.

Saving Mystery, liberating, freeing,
In you we live and move and have our being.

48 *

WISDOM INCARNATE
remembering Jesus

Sophia Creator, Wise Spirit Parent of us all,
    we thank you for sending to us your Wisdom Incarnate, Jesus
        of Nazareth,[51]
    and for linking us to the community of believers
        that, following him, connects us to a religious heritage
        going back to Moses and the Hebrew Prophets,
        our sisters and brothers in faith and ritual.
Come, incarnate your Wisdom and Mercy in us also,
    that we may be worthy inheritors of the promise of the Torah,
    giving to our children
        an inheritance of reverence for life and diversity
        enriched by our own experiences, both of joy and of sorrow.

God of History, liberating, freeing,
In you we live and move and have our being.

49 *

CO-WORKERS WITH YOU
when needing inspiration

Holy Mystery, She Who Is,
    we are hoping to be co-workers with your burning flame of
        Wisdom
    and to be sacraments of your liberating heart,[52]
    knowing that it is through the breakable bread of our own time
        and energy
    that your Communioning Wisdom and Strength
      will draw together the faith communities
        that can become divine and messianic hands and feet
        and co-creators of a new, fully just human society.
Make use of us
    as you made use of your servant Jesus
    for the purposes of your incomprehensible Wisdom.

Mystery God, empowering and freeing,
In you we live and move and have our being.

MOTHER GOD

· VI ·

. . . womb-love for us . . .

The prophet Hosea depicts God as saying about
sinful people, "My heart turns over within me,
my compassion grows warm and tender" (ll:8).
The word "compassion," when broken down to
its root, means to suffer with, to feel with: God
here is anything but cold and distant. In relation
to insights of feminist theology, biblical scholars
are pointing out that the root word for
compassion in Hebrew is the same as the root
word for woman's womb *(rhm)*. To say that God
has compassion on us is literally to say that God
has **womb-love for us** and loves us the way a
mother loves the child of her womb. . . .

Elizabeth A. Johnson, *Consider Jesus,* p. 117

50 *

HUMAN MOTHERS
thinking of God as Divine Mother

Holy Loving Spirit,
    we reach toward you through all that you have made:
    you enliven creation, you give it its character.
Since women are, like men, images of God,
    what you give to human mothers, for instance,
    wonderfully sketches, though faintly, your being:
    a birth-giving, nurturance, play and delight in the other,
    unmerited love, fierce protectiveness,
    compassion, forgiveness,
    courage, service, and care for the weak and vulnerable.
Motherhood at its best exemplifies all these
    and shows forth an image
    of your own mysteriously indulgent ways.[53]

Parenting Spirit, present, loving, freeing,
In you we live and move and have our being.

51 *

MAKING ROOM
praising the God who gave us birth

Holy Mystery, in a true sense
   you have hollowed out a place for us, as it were, within
      yourself.
We are never swallowed up in your infinity,
   but have our distinct existence within your own.
In this your self-limitation and self-emptying
      to make room for your creation
   we perceive your very essence:
   the same kenosis or "self-emptying"
   which was paradigmatically enacted in Christ Jesus,
   and is consonantly re-enacted in every mother
      who makes room for another in her womb.
Mothering Mystery,
   we give thanks that we have known you at last, if ever so
      slightly.
Blessed be She who spoke and the world became.
Blessed be She Who Is.
Blessed be She who will be eternally unable to abandon her
      children,
   even long after their human life is through.[54]
Blessed be She Who Is.

Sophia, She Who Is, empowering, freeing,
In you we will forever have our being.

52 *

MAKING A DIFFERENCE
joy in God's presence

We rejoice to realize that this world and ourselves
   make a difference to you, Creating Mystery:
   without creatures like ourselves
   you would not be *our* beloved creator, vivifier,
      redeemer, liberator, companion, and future.
We matter to you like the child of your womb: infinitely,
      unforgettably.[55]
Whatever the future may bring, we put our trust in you.

Sophia Mystery, present, caring, freeing,
In you we live and move and have our being.

53 ✳

UNCONDITIONAL LOVE

when feeling thankful

Mothering God, Mysterious She Who Is,
    we do not have to be wonderful according to external norms
        to win your love,
    for it is freely given by virtue of your maternal relationship
        with us.
Motherlike, you look upon us,
    through no merit of our own,
    with a love that makes us beautiful and a pleasure to you.
We shall always be beautiful in your sight,
    for your vision of us makes us all that we are.[56]
Could it be that your link to us is as strong, appreciative, and
        forgiving
    as is the link between a mother and the child of her womb?
We give thanks.

Maternal Spirit, present, loving, freeing,
In you we live and move and have our being.

54 *

YOUR MATERNAL LOVE
cooperating with God

As creative, life-giving Mother of all that is,
   you, Creator Spirit, have at heart the well-being of the whole
      world,
   its life-systems and all its inhabitants.
It is your maternally interested love we make present
   whenever we work to preserve the earth's resources
   and endangered species,
   rightly reordering economic relationships within the human
      family,
   equitably redistributing goods
   and banning whatever damages and defiles creation.[57]
Sweep our hearts into your life-preserving projects.
Make us incarnations of your caring Wisdom.

Sophia, She Who Is, empowering, freeing,
In you we live and move and have our being.

55 *

YOU ARE BEYOND

when reaching toward Holy Mystery

Sophia-God, Mother Creator of inexhaustible mystery,
   you are beyond and within the world;
   behind, with, and ahead of us;
   above, alongside, and around us.
While in you we live and have our being,
   like still-embryonic children,
   we know almost nothing of you
   where you are God in the fullness of incomprehensible
      possibility.[58]
Give us patience with the darkness of this world,
   and hope in a brighter world to come.

Mothering Mystery, loving, guiding, freeing,
In you we live and move and have our being.

56 *

NURTURING WOMB
thinking of God as our all

Holy Womb of the world
   from which we are born again each moment,
   and within which we grow, awaiting our birth into eternal life;
Womb-love,[59] caring motheringness, steadfast fatheringness,
Incomprehensible God, the One Who Is,
   we are not only born from you at our life-spark's beginning
     and at each moment of being and life,
   but it is from you we get the nourishment our being needs
     each instant:
   milk and bread, yes, and air to breathe,
   but also thought, right judgment, mercy, faith;
   and good anger, discomfort and resistance as well:
     anger along with you that the weak are misled and
       manipulated,
     discomfort with the status quo that leaves millions out,
     resistance to the momentum of a culture
      of privilege, violence, and destitution.
Give us the hearts of parents also whose offspring and kin
   are all the inhabitants of this planet and cosmos.
See our faith. Enlarge our compassion. Help our unbelief.

Creating Parent God, empowering, freeing,
In you we live and move and have our being.

57 ✳

MATERNAL POWER

feeling one with the earth

Mother of the Universe who dwells in bright darkness,
    we who are creatures of the one earth,
        all the human race, the animal kingdom,
        every growing thing, all the continents and oceans,
        the atmosphere and the fertile mantle
are siblings from the same womb,
    your brood and kin.
Your cosmic maternal voice
    cries out in terrible laments to give birth to an ever new
        creation
and to overcome whatever might destroy it.[60]
Safe in your perfect care, Holy Wisdom,
    we rejoice in hope and entrust ourselves to your mystery.

Creator Mother, birthing, feeding, freeing,
In you we live and move and have our being.

58 *

YOUR MYSTERY

probing the mystery of She Who Is

Holy Wisdom, you are mystery beyond all telling:
   but through the image of mothering
   we reach into the depth of your mysteriousness,
     naming you as unoriginate origin, primordial being,
     hidden source of all that is,
     creator without beginning yet ever young and fresh,
     absolutely free, fount of outpouring goodness, root of life.[61]
As we grow from your root, pour forth from your goodness,
   and exist from your existence,
    grace us with vitality to help build the created world
     according to your dreams.

God, our Origin, inspiring, freeing,
In you we live and move and have our being.

59 ✱

LIKE A WIND
welcoming Holy Mystery

Great Spirit, Creator Mother of the World,
    like a wind you seem to be always drawing near and passing by
    to empower your creatures toward life and well-being
    in the teeth of the antagonistic structures in our political
        reality.[62]
Welcome, Spirit of hope!
Welcome, Sophia-Wisdom!
Welcome, Empowering Strength,
    She Who Is and will always be, free, loving, infinitely creative.

Holy God, empowering and freeing,
In you we live and move and have our being.

60 *

RELATIONSHIP OF SOLIDARITY
toward union with God

Spirit-Sophia,
    friend, sister, brother, father, mother, and grandmother of the
        world,
    enlighten us so that we may be able to build
    a relationship of solidarity and friendship with you,
    then expand our hearts to a caring concern
        for all the created world around us.
We are loved by you in order to love others,
    gifted in order to give gifts,
    befriended in order to relate to all the world as friends.
May it become so in our lives.[63]

God of Love, mysterious and freeing,
In you we live and move and have our being.

61 *

INEXHAUSTIBLE LIVINGNESS
the Presence always there

Holy God,
  your mystery is incomprehensible.
All the astonishing action of your Spirit in history,
  promoting and supporting us
    amid the dialectical ups and downs of freedom,
    the Spirit of your Wisdom walking through time
    in the history and destiny of Jesus called the Christ—
  these, we know, are not provisional mysteries
  able to be cleared up at some future moment
  such as at our personal death or the end of the world.
Your divine goodness is absolute mystery.
It is of your very essence as God so to *be*
  that human minds can never exhaust your livingness
  as it is poured out on all creation.[64]
In this light our living and our prayer may be
  an endless spiritual adventure.
We give thanks.

God within, mysterious and freeing,
In you we live and move and have our being.

· VII ·

. . . a robust, appropriate name for God . . .

Naming toward God from the perspective of women's dignity, I suggest a feminist gloss on this highly influential text (Ex 3:14 "I am who I am"). In English the "who" of *qui est* (in the Latin bible) is open to inclusive interpretation, and this indicates a way to proceed. If God is not intrinsically male, if women are truly created in the image of God, if being female is an excellence, if what makes women exist as women in all difference is participation in divine being, then there is cogent reason to name toward Sophia-God, "the one who is," with implicit reference to an antecedent of the grammatically and symbolically feminine gender. SHE WHO IS can be spoken as **a robust, appropriate name for God.** With this name we bring to bear in a female metaphor all the power carried in the ontological symbol of absolute, relational liveliness that energizes the world. . . .

Elizabeth A. Johnson, *She Who Is*, p. 243

62 *

LIGHTEN MY HEART
when reaching for joy

Loving God, mothering creator, She Who Is,
   lighten my heart with the sweet beauty of this life
   so that in my joy and my enjoyment,
   you can also know a joy for having given me birth,
      given me my personal selfhood and being,
      and set me down to live
      in this land of mystery, challenge, and possibility.[65]

Creating Mother, loving, guiding, freeing,
In you we live and move and have our being.

63 ∗

knowing the need for She Who Is

It is you, Sophia, She Who Is,
    who are "above all and through all and in all" (Eph. 4:6),
    and we easily attest to your presence in the midst of beauty.
We also lean on the strength of your presence
    in the midst of struggle and suffering,
    and we mourn your absence when bewildering evil
    seems to cast your nearness into the dark.[66]
Inspire us all to perseverance in hope,
    to risk-taking in crying out for justice,
    and to the fullness of faith and trust in you.

Empowering God, inspiring, strengthening, freeing,
In you we live and move and have our being.

64 *

RELATIONAL MYSTERY
thinking of God's desires

Holy Sophia, She Who Is,
    you are the relational mystery of life
    who desires the liberated human existence of all people made in
        your image,
    who desires the enlightened development of all our human
        race,
    and inspires in us today a new caringness for our earthly
        home.[67]
Fill our hearts with your desires
    so we can participate fully in a communal human destiny,
    worthy of your loving plan.

Creating Mystery, gifting, leading, freeing,
In you we live and move and have our being.

65 *

FUNCTIONING IMAGES
finding God everywhere

My God, named in our Latin Scriptures as *Qui-Est,*
    the One Who Is, She Who Is, He Who Is,
      everything around us is in some way an image of you,
      from our colossal oceans, to the human hearts we most admire,
      from the unthinkably intricate and infinitesimal atoms and
        forces,
      to the faces of children bursting with energy and promise,
      along with an astonishing animal kingdom
      and an almost unbelievably elaborate cosmos mostly unknown.
It all images you.
Give us always enough light to see your face beneath each
    creation
    as each image "functions" in our minds
    to reveal your holy mystery and who we, your creatures, are.[68]
Come, invade our minds with your bright darkness,
Mysterious Spirit utterly beyond our imaginings.

Unknown Mystery God, inspiring, freeing,
In you we live and move and have our being.

66 *

TRANSCENDENT MATRIX
honoring She Who Is

You, Holy Wisdom, She Who Is,
    live as the transcendent matrix
    who underlies and supports all existence and potential for new
        being,
    all resistance to oppression
    and to the powers that stand against justice and reverence for
        the earth.[69]
May I go my way in confidence and optimism,
    knowing that, as long as I carry your gift of existence,
    you are with me, near me, within me, around me,
    providing me the potential
        for enlightenment, perseverance, and liberation.

Creating Spirit, present, loving, freeing,
In you we live and move and have our being.

67 *

WHAT WE KNOW
asking who God is

What do we know of you, Holy Mystery?
　　You are the inconceivable power who gives life and design to
　　　　the world,
　　　　sustains it everywhere and always,
　　　　joins its crucified history through your compassionate
　　　　　　womb-love,
　　　　empowers every event of healing and liberation,
　　　　and is that deepest mystery toward which the world moves.[70]
Holy Wisdom, She Who Is, it is joy to be your invention
　　and your companion.
Give us the grace to live in your presence,
　　exhilarated by your nearness,
　　rooted in an enlightened and inclusive humanism,
　　and linked in intimacy with people we love and care about.

Creating Mystery, God, befriending, freeing,
In you we live and move and have our being.

68 *

MIDWIFE GOD

when looking back on our life

Creating God,
   did you not know me before I knew myself?
Was it not your skilled hands that helped guide me
   in my emerging from my own mother's womb?[71]
You were there, Sophia! Compassionate She Who Is!
Before I awoke to selfhood,
   when I was still unable to speak (for I had no thoughts),
   when I was as yet unable
   to know the meaning of those comforting sounds
     that surrounded me as an infant,
   yet knew I was cared for lovingly,
you were there
   under it all, guiding it all,
   inspiring it all, designing it all,
   destining it all toward the self I am and am yet to become.
I give thanks for your dynamically interacting presence,
   vibrantly communioning, invisible-to-me Presence,
   still the midwife of all that comes about in and through me.
Make me a midwife of all who turn to me in need or solidarity.

Sophia, Mystery, caring, helping, freeing,
In you we live and move and have our being.

69 ✳

THIS NEW MOMENT

facing responsibility for change

Help us, Holy Mystery, with the consequences of our task—
    to alleviate the dominance of the patriarchal paradigm of God
    which is so detrimental to your image on earth
       and to the well-being of human community.[72]
We give thanks for this new moment
    when, by the force of study and of inspired communal action
    there is unveiled your new face, Holy God,
    the face of a God in whose image women—as well as men—
       are created
    and in whose mystery they are reflected
       with new sacred names that point to this image:
    Holy Wisdom, Sophia, Creator Mother, Mothering Spirit,
    the one incomprehensible triune God, She Who Is.
We give thanks for the way these new images and names
       function.
For once we come to see our male messiah, Jesus,
    as an incarnation of Sophia, the Wisdom of God,
    as "the prophet of She Who Is,"
    then we can sense a gender-inclusive framework
    which removes the male emphasis in our traditions
    that so quickly turn to dominance and elitism.[73]

World-circling Mystery, loving, guiding, freeing,
In you we live and move and have our being.

O God,
save what your right hand has planted. Psalm 80

· VIII ·

. . . a trinitarian existence . . .

As we trace the vivifying ways of the Spirit, the
compassionate, liberating story of Jesus-Sophia,
and the generative mystery of the Creator
Mother, it becomes clear that the Christian
experience of the one God is multifaceted. The
God of inexhaustible mystery who is
inexpressibly other is also with the world in the
flesh of history, and is furthermore closer to us
than we are to ourselves. Sophia-God is beyond,
with, and within the world; behind, with, and
ahead of us; above, alongside, and around us.
The religious experience of being met in this
diversity of saving ways functioned historically
and continues to be the starting point for seeking
the intelligibility of speech about God in the
Christian tradition. Shaped by this encounter,
thought discerns a distinct kind of monotheism:
the one God enjoys **a trinitarian existence.** . . .

Elizabeth A. Johnson, *She Who Is*, p. 191

70 *

SHEER ALIVENESS
exploring God's inner life

Holy Mystery, She Who Is,
    you are the one whose very nature is sheer aliveness, joy, and
        vitality.
We accept from our tradition
    the threeness of your inner life:
    Father, Word, Spirit; Mother, Wisdom, Energy.
You are the profoundly relational source
    of the being of the whole universe,
    and everything you make carries with it
    the distinguishing mark of your inner life: relatedness.
It is our joy to realize
    that therefore nothing and no one is alone, left out, or
        unrelated.
This is our faith
    and in it we give more trust to what exists
    than we can really explain, justify, or understand.[74]
We pray for aliveness also,
    and for that ebullience and lightheartedness that wells up in
        our spirits
    when we feel your comforting nearness.
We instinctively turn to you as our compassionate Creator Spirit,
    and we submit to the unknowing and to the darkness in your
        mystery.

Triune God, creating, leading, freeing,
In you we live and move and have our being.

71 *

YOUR WAYS

in awe of the ways of God

Gracious Creating Spirit,
   your ways in the world are multifaceted.
As Spirit-Sophia you blow like the wind where you will,
   pervading the world with vitalizing and liberating power,
   bringing divine presence in the world to its widest universality.
As Jesus-Sophia, you inspire our Messiah to preach the nearness
     of your reign,
   embodying in his heart your divine caringness for the poor and
     outcast,
   and incarnating the divine self-emptying in his life sacrifice,
   as well as delivering to us a divine promise in the doctrine of
     his resurrection.[75]
As Holy Wisdom and unoriginate Mother of all things,
   you uphold the world
     as its sustaining source of being
     and potential for change and for new being.
We worship you. We give you thanks.
   We praise you for your wonders.

Triune Holy Mystery, caring, freeing,
In you we live and move and have our being.

72 *

A HOLY THREENESS
wondering at God's Mystery

Holy Wisdom and Creative Mystery,
    what can we know of your inner life?
Our traditions suggest in you a holy threeness
    existing in mutual coinherence,
    the dancing around together of Spirit, Wisdom, and Mother;[76]
    or of mutual Love, Love from Love, and unoriginate Love,
    pouring itself out into creation, vitalizing everything that
        exists,
    including ourselves.
How dense your triune mystery!
How bright your blinding darkness!

Holy Three, One God, inspiring, freeing,
In you we live and move and have our being.

73 *

TRIUNE GOD
praying to the God of relationship

How shall we speak, Holy God,
  of your inner relatedness, of your triune mystery?
We might think of your threeness
  as Unoriginate Mother, beloved Child, and the Spirit of your
    mutual love.
Or we might think of you as the immense vitality of
  Wisdom-Sophia,
  her personal Word
  and her incomprehensible Energies.
Or as one Eternal Communion of a triune mystery,
  hidden, then uttered, then bestowed.
In whatever way we may turn our minds toward this mystery,
  we instinctively know your presence is not distant or
    theoretical
  but close-by, consonant with what we know of true
    communitarian life,
  and overflowing with relationship within and without.[77]
We worship your inexhaustible communion, Holy Mystery,
  and give thanks for all our own links with others.

Communioning Sophia, living, freeing,
In you we live and move and have our being.

74 *

COMFORTING PRESENCE
having faith in She Who Is

Holy Spirit, your triune livingness is ever a comforting thought:
  you are an eternal communioning of relationships,
  mysterious, present, and given to us.[78]
Despite all your unknown-ness, this we know:
  you are not solitary, alone, ruling in sovereign singleness and
    privilege,
  unapproachable, monarchical, nor—as you are so often
    imagined—male.
  There is often something fearful in each of these attributes.
  We can put those fears away.
You present yourself to our prophets and seers—and thus to us—
  as relational, mysteriously multiple in your inner life,
  unimaginably dynamic within yourself, as a community in
    mystery,
  a holy *koinonia*,
  and therefore everywhere vital in a way that is comfortable to
    us.
We really should not fear to go to you at life's end,
  for you, despite your mystery, remain an intimate, a familiar,
    God.
  As we find ourselves relational beings, so we find you also.
  We are your children and thus we resemble you.
  We have been yours from the very beginning
    so nothing about us is unfamiliar or foreign or surprising to
      you.
Intimate yet unfathomable Mystery,
  grace us with this faith forever,
  literally, forever, and forever.
We may suffer temporary defeats, setbacks, illnesses, failures;
  but our faith tells us these will be only pauses.
  In the end, the very end, we know in whom we have believed:
  our God, our home, our home at last![79]

Triune Parent God, inspiring, freeing,
In you we live and move and have our being.

75 *

AN INNER CIRCLING
bewildered by the Holy Mystery

Holy Mystery, your trinity points
    to an inner divine life circling around an unimaginable convivial
        relation,
    a loving God, pouring out goodness and life and being
        in incomprehensible richness of possibility and creation.[80]
Give us the joy of a convivial circle of our own,
    the laughter of mutual acceptance,
    and lighthearted appreciation our ever-surprising diversity.
Be our God, Holy Communioning Spirit.

Divine Communion, present, leading, freeing,
In you we live and move and have our being.

76 *

DRAW ME
when needing God's presence

Dancing, Communioning Sophia Mystery,
    draw me into the circle of understanding
    where I can be aware of your presence,
    realize your care for me,
    and feel confidence in the strength you have
    to empower me throughout my life.[81]
Give me both the gift of joy and compassion,
    of care for both the global commonwealth and for our planet
       home.
Help thou my unbelief:
    it is only part of the questioning heart you have created within
       me.

Creating Trinity, inspiring, freeing,
In you we live and move and have our being.

77 ✳

HOLY COMMUNION, OUR GOD
imagining God's heart

Holy One, You Who Are,
   being-in-communion constitutes your very essence,[82]
   a free communion always going forth and always receiving in,
   a mystery of personal connectedness
      that constitutes the very livingness of your holy life.
Give us a constant awareness of your caring mystery,
   and an enjoyment of the vitality of your triune communion.

Spirit Communion, giving, gracing, freeing,
In you we live and move and have our being.

78 *

HEART OF ALL REALITY
finding the heart of reality

Holy God,
in your trinitarian life we come to see
that divine relatedness is the heart of all reality,
a relatedness of genuine mutuality in which there is radical
equality.[83]
In the light of this understanding,
give us hope for a world of connections, communication, and
rootedness,
a reflection of your own inner life and joy.

Communioning Spirit, living, loving, freeing,
In you we live and move and have our being.

79 ✳

TRINITARIAN FAITH

peering within the Divine Mystery

You, Holy God, are Spirit-Sophia,
   the mobile, pure, people-loving Spirit
   who pervades every wretched corner of the earth,
   wailing at the waste, releasing power that enables fresh starts.
   Your energy quickens the earth to life,
      your beauty shines in the stars,
      your strength breaks forth
      in every fragment of shalom, real justice and renewal
      that transpires in arenas of violence and meaninglessness.
From generation to generation you enter into holy souls,
      and into not so holy ones also,
      to make them friends of God and prophets,
      thereby making human beings allies of your redeeming
          purpose.
You dwell in the world at its center and at its edges,
      an active vitality crying out in labor, birthing a new creation.
Among your signs are fire, wind, water, and all color: in fact
      everything splendid and sparkling and awe-inspiring.
You, Sophia, are also in Jesus the Christ, your child and prophet
and in Jesus we see you
personally pitching your tent in the flesh of humanity
      to teach the paths of justice.
The shape of your love for the world, Holy Wisdom,
      is the shape of the historical life of our crucified prophet,
         who defeats death:
      a love both wise and unselfish,
      both patiently reasonable and sacrificing of self for the sake
         of justice.
You, Sophia-God, are irreversibly connected
      with the joy and anguish of human history,
      in the flesh of both our prophet and of ourselves.
In your power, Jesus now takes on a new communal identity
      as the Risen Cosmic Messiah,
      the body and unity of all those women and men

who share in the transformation of the world
through compassionate, delighting, and suffering love.
In solidarity with his memory, and empowered by the same
Spirit,
we, his little flock, become configured
into a sacrament of the world's salvation,
and are empowered to shape new communities
of freedom and solidarity.
You, Holy God, are an unimaginable abyss of livingness,
a Holy Wisdom both unknown and unknowable,
matrix/womb of all that exists,
mother and fashioner of all things
who yourself dwell in light inaccessible.
You are a hidden God,
bent on the world's healing and liberation
despite all of history's reversals and defeats.[84]
We give you our human worship and gratitude.

Triune Spirit God, creating, freeing,
In you we live and move and have our being.

· IX ·

. . . *in the midst of distress* . . .

Speaking about SHE WHO IS in the dynamic terms of mutual and equal trinitarian relations and the essence of liveliness opens the door anew to ancient language about the divine pathos or involvement in the suffering of the world. **In the midst of distress** religious experience at times senses the presence of Sophia-God drawing near and accompanying people down the dark road of pain; at other times the intuition of faith finds that God has already passed by and is terrifyingly absent. What is the right way to speak about God in the constant happening of woe? Are human beings the only ones who weep and groan, or can this also be predicated of the holy mystery of God who cherishes the beloved world. . . ?

Elizabeth A. Johnson, *She Who Is*, p. 246

80 *

GOD IN PAIN

wanting to console She Who Is

Mystifying Divinity, existing beyond all our names for you,
  how is it possible that you are close to us and are still God,
  for if you are really close by,
  in all your compassion for our race there would inevitably be
     suffering
  and how can a God suffer?

Were you only "He Who Is," perhaps we might imagine you
     above pain;[85]
  but since you are also "She Who Is,"
  it becomes unthinkable that you would not be in pain
  in solidarity with all your beloved who are in pain.
Holy One in agony,
  yet encompassing all the world's joy as well,
  give us hearts of faith
  so we can find you
  in the depths of this dark light.

Creator Mother, loving, caring, freeing,
In you we live and move and have our being.

81 *

PAIN TRANSFORMED

when partnering God

We are honored to be present to you,
Holy Compassionate Communioning Mystery,
   witnessing in faith the strength of your compassionate love
   as it enters the pain of the world
   to transform it from within with the force of moral
      indignation,[86]
   concern for a broken creation,
   and a growingly communal thirst for justice.
All our names for you fall short of your mystery,
   but among our verbal symbols that name-toward you,
   we may choose to call you She Who Is:
   for thus we get a sense
      of both your fierce caring for each and all of your children,
   and of your vulnerable empathy with all our human sorrows.
You are also He Who Is and The One Who Is,
   each pointing to another set of imaginative gateways
   toward your mystery.
Guide our hearts to yourself, Holy Womb of all beginnings
   and our welcoming Home at last.

Sophia, She Who Is, empowering, freeing,
In you we live and move and have our being.

82 *

YOU SUFFER?

seeking a God almost beyond belief

Sophia-Wisdom, Dynamic Unfathomable Creating Mystery,
   is it possible that you are really in solidarity with all who
      suffer?[87]
Can it be you have not abandoned them—as it seems?
How is it possible you care terribly
   that they have so little peace of mind,
   so little confidence they will have food for another day,
   so little security against illness, attack, homelessness, and
      hatred?
How is it possible for you to be God,
   and to be unable to alleviate our pain?
Help me reformulate my concept of the divine.
Inexhaustible Mystery,
   are you limited to doing what Love can do?
   I long to give you my faith and trust.
   Help thou my unbelief.

Unknowable Mystery, present, loving, freeing,
In you we live and move and have our being.

83 ✳

INFINITE YOUR SUFFERING
when mystified by pain

Precisely because you are infinite, Holy One,
 is not your divine suffering infinite and beyond human
   comprehension?[88]
 Do you not also need comforting?
In fact you are not—as was our limited God of exclusively male
 qualities—
 impassible, unrelated to our race,
 an all-dominant divinity "willing" everything that happens
 or at least, like a dominant Lord, actively permitting it to
   happen.
There is no such divinity; "he" would be a moral scandal.
We know you exist as our all-compassionate Creator,
 and you care infinitely;
 but how that can be in view of all that is evil around us,
 we are unable to explain.
With Job, we put our hand over our mouth.

Baffling Mystery God, empowering, freeing,
In you we live and move and have our being.

84 *

finding a way forward

In the midst of disaster, in every time of grief,
    we only find a way forward in finding you also, Creator
        Wisdom, in grief;
    and it is often your grief—as well as our own—that awakens
        protest.[89]
Grace us with protesting hearts
    when injustice prevails and despair tempts us all,
    when greed wins the day in arrogant self-aggrandizement,
    and a human person at work is considered a commodity.
You are the Mystery to whom we turn in time of sorrow and
        alienation,
    just as we also make you a part of our victories and joys.
Be ever a part of our Life
    as we forever are a part of yours.

Wisdom, empathizing, loving, freeing,
In you we live and move and have our being.

85 *

SUFFERING IN GOD
feeling God in pain

Sophia-God,
    your divine suffering is your act of love
    freely overflowing in compassion for all in pain.
    Since you care for us infinitely, your pain for our pain is
        unlimited.
We grieve with you, Holy Mystery, in all of creation's sorrow,
    as we rejoice with you in all human joy, invention, and
        promise.[90]
Guide our hearts into paths of justice and human solidarity.

Compassionate Mystery, caring, helping, freeing,
In you we live and move and have our being.

86 *

WOMB DARKNESS
when peering through the dark

Unimaginable Communion of Creating Energy, Wisdom, and
    Caringness,
    why are we humans so incomplete, so illusion-prone and unwise,
    given to self-defeating competitiveness,
    so easily defeated and disappointed, so ridiculously
        individualistic?
Could it be simply because we are somehow embryonic,
    that we have long months of growth ahead, as it were,
    before we shall be born?
When we call you "Womb of the World,"
    She-Who-Is—in whom we live and move and have our being,
    we discover a useful image:
    we live in womb-darkness.
Darkness and incompleteness is our natural, if temporary, state.
To live therefore in the naked light would be impossible:
    we are not yet ready.
Our daily work, to build up the God's commonwealth
    in the shadowy world around and within us,
    is simply the natural process
    of becoming the fully formed body of humanity, awaiting birth.
Once we explained our darkened mind and ineffectual will
    as supposedly the result of an "original sin"
    for which our limitations are the punishment.
Perhaps here we come upon a more helpful image than that:
    the natural embryonic process we know in human gestation.
Using this paradigm, then, it is not "sin" that limits us:
    it is just nature's good, if mysterious, process.
Holy Womb of all that is and is to be,[91]
    we hesitantly rejoice in our darkness,
    we tolerate our agonies and pain, our bewilderment and
        unknowingness,
    for we believe in your maternal processes
    even while understanding them as little as we do.

Sophia God, mysterious and freeing,
In you we live and move and have our being.

87 ✳

laying our hopes on God

Unnamable One, our God,
  can you lead us into the community of shalom and justice?
That is your desire, that is your constant longing
  and it is our own greatest destiny as well.
You urge each of us from within to become our full selves,[92]
  following our gifts wherever they may lead,
  connecting to others and rooting ourselves
    in the human circle of which we are most naturally a part.
Inspire us and guide us today
  as you have inspired your people of every age.
We are on your side, by your grace.
That is where we always long to be:
  on the side of life, of liberation into a community of equals,
  of worthy work for all, of adequate and dignified shelter,
  of a planet home healed and respected,
  of nourishment, of growth in every human way,
  toward insight, discovery, peace, joy, caringness, and health.
Be with us in all our desires and undertakings.

Peace-giving Mystery, loving, guiding, freeing,
In you we live and move and have our being.

MASS MURDER TORTURE
SEXISM POVERTY
WAR ILLNESS
RACISM
NATUR-
AL DIS-
ASTER
INJUST-
ICE
DESTRUC-
TION OF
THE EARTH

Jean Morningstar, snjm '94

I drench you with my tears.

Isaiah 16:9

106

· X ·

. . . *the dark horizon* . . .

It's when the second hand is ticking around my
watch and I am plodding from task to heavy
task, just holding my world together so another
hour can come about, that I feel those futile
doubts: those doubts I wish I did not have to
have. Is it worth it? Am I achieving anything? Is
there hope after yesterday's tragedies? Then I
almost haven't time to believe, no time for a
vision or a hope or a prayer.

But when I'm touched with wonder, then I can
begin to believe and not to doubt. It happens
when I see a courage and beauty that seems
greater than human, when I see plain humanity
but suspect inSpiration, when I hear a harmony
among impossibly disparate sounds, when the
grace of a series of events so take me by surprise
that I cannot not pay attention.

It's when events like these revive a deep hope
beneath my own despair that I begin to doubt
my worthless doubts, to doubt that some
doubting is really wise or justified, when I may
live for a moment in faith and glimpse a faraway
land of light as small as a star on **the dark
horizon** of my inner world.

William Cleary, *A Doubter's Prayerbook*, p. 16

88 ✱

ANOTHER KIND OF POWER
when in need of hope

Holy God, we will not say you are all powerful,
    or alternatively, a god of limited power.
It is another *kind* of power we find in you:
    neither power-over nor powerlessness,
    but something akin to power-with:
    relational, persuasive, erotic in its connectedness,
    loving, playful, empowering, resisting.[93]
Your power-with is infinite,
    filling us with energy to resist evil
      and to build the human and earthly project,
    to lay hold of our full dignity, and to guide us to
    —and through and beyond—
    death in our efforts toward building freedom and a just world.
Your empowering strength heals our brokenheartedness
    and fills us with an inexplicable hope
    that is stronger than evil, stronger than disappointment,
    stronger even than death.

Empowering God, compassionate and freeing,
In you we live and move and have our being.

89 *

YOURS THE POWER
looking toward God in hope

Yours, Holy Mystery, She Who Is, our Creator, is endless
    power-with:
  yours is the power of person-making among those diminished
      by pain
    who do not know their own dignity;
  yours the grace of conversion
    to turn from dead-end ways and walk the path of newness of
      life;
  yours the light of conscience;
  yours the power to shake up assured certainties
    and introduce the grace of a new question;
  yours the wisdom to foment discomfort among the unduly
    comfortable;
  yours the oil of gladness
    enjoyed in experiences that heal, refresh, and invigorate;
  yours the vigor that energizes the fire of active, outgoing
    love.[94]
We worship you. We give you thanks. We praise you for your
  wonders.

Empowering Mystery, loving, gifting, freeing,
In you we live and move and have our being.

90 *

JOINING IN YOUR WRATH
when entering the heart of God

Holy Caringness and Wisdom,
    we join in your wrath
    over the abuse of the vulnerable in this world.[95]
Sophia, Holy Energy and Love,
    we also join in your joy
    over the pleasure that thrives in the hearts and bodies
    of so many living creatures.
Holy Communion of Wisdom, Energy, and Caringness,
    draw us into communion with you
    as we live through the mysteries of evil and good
    that surround us every day.

Sophia, Mystery, loving, caring, freeing,
In you we live and move and have our being.

91 ∗

NEW FAITH LEVEL
searching for the real God

Protect the human community,
    Sacred Mystery within us and around us,
  from the self-blinding idolatry
  that has sometimes been a hindrance
    to our communal religious quest:
  using for you exclusively male words and symbols.
That god-image is of a lesser god![96]
  He has eyes that never see,
  ears that never hear,
  lips that never speak.[97]
True God!
  whom we can know of if we will take time with the world's
    mysteries,
  She Who Is, He Who Is, The One Who Is,
  our human race rises to a new level of faith
    once we name you for our God.
  Then we will have
  in addition to a God who is Father-like, King-like, and Lord-
    like
  also a God with all the compassion and caringness of a mother,
  a God with a sister's heart for us all,
  with the unfailing support of a wise and compassionate
    Grandmother,
  a God with perhaps less than the almighty power
    which an ideal male divinity must have
  but with an irresistible strength
    like that of committed and united women and men
    through the centuries of our experience.
Fill us with this strength, Holy Mystery!

Spirit Mystery God, creating, freeing,
In you we live and move and have our being.

92 *

giving thanks for something new

Divine Mystery, Sophia-God,
   let me participate in this new moment in religious history--
   when women are at last voicing their own experience of you
     and enriching our thought-world
       with genuinely new words and symbols,
     reflecting more fully the revelation
       of your mysterious and incomprehensible Being.
Sophia Wisdom,
Divine Mother in whom we live and move and have our being:
   the whole world warms with this new light and heat.
We feel your Divine Being with us in an entirely new way,[98]
   no longer only as Lord God, Heavenly King,
   Generous Father, Caring Brother, Companioning Inner Spirit:
   but imaged as well in all we know of female persons—
   and that is an entirely new world of knowledge,
   as different and newly revelatory
     as women are different from men.
Let me participate in this new world of enlightenment,
   as dark and dense as are all images of your holy mystery.

Sophia God, empowering and freeing,
In you we live and move and have our being.

93 *

LINKED TO YOU
believing She is there

Holy Living God,
    your presence points to the absolute future,
    present intrinsically in the world throughout its history—
    as that which provides its ultimate consummation.
You are in the world as ground, inspiration, and goal of all our
      struggles.[99]
We know your presence
    when we stop a moment to ground ourselves in reality.
We feel your presence also when something in your creation
    suddenly overawes us.
But we are most linked to your passionate caring presence
    when we join the struggle for justice and freedom,
    whether we know you explicitly in the midst of it or not.

Dynamic God, empowering and freeing,
In you we live and move and have our being.

94 *

NOTHING TO FEAR
when calling out to God

Fire of Sheer Aliveness,
    whose act of being overflows and we suddenly exist!
    In our precarious existence, we give thanks for your
        unquenchable life.
    Even in our distress we may proclaim:
The One-Who-Is gives us being! We need not be afraid!
She-Who-Is surrounds and supports us:
    we can go from strength to strength in the presence of her
        strength. [100]
In You we have our being:
    what have we to fear?
Help us dare to accept the challenge
    to partner you, Holy God, in working for justice and
        shalom, [101]
    lighthearted in accepting our own clownish inadequacies,
    often so incongruously bent on impossible tasks.
In your strength all things are possible.

Creative Mystery, loving, guarding, freeing,
In you we live and move and have our being.

95 ✳

when God seems distant

You, Holy Mystery,
    are the Communion in which we live and move and have our
       being,
    the Mystery growing ever more mysterious[102]
    as we contemplate the paradoxes of your Being:
        multiple in your manifestations yet a unity,
        yet incomprehensible as a unity
        since we seem to live within a conflict between
        good and evil.
Incomprehensible God,
    be with us as we dare to take up the struggle to understand
    and live in faith within your Mystery.

Empowering Presence, guiding, loving, freeing,
In you we live and move and have our being.

96 *

in awe of God's wrath

Your wrath, Holy Mystery, against injustice
  is not the opposite of mercy but its co-relative.[103]
Your wrath is a mode of caring response in the face of evil,
  aroused by what is mean or shameful
    or injurious to beloved human beings and the created world
      itself.
Your wrath precisely because you care with a love that goes
    beyond our imagining
  is likewise immeasurable.
Empower us, Holy Mystery, with your just anger and boundless
    anguish.
We join in your divine mourning
  which goes forth to include the whole suffering world,
  even to those who appear to be our enemies.[104]
May even those morally alienated from you
  know true joy and peace in harmonizing at last
  with the music of your infinite desires.

Compassionate Mystery, caring, guiding, freeing,
In you we live and move and have our being.

· XI ·

. . . *the grace to shout* . . .

Today we ask
the grace to shout
when it hurts,
even though silence is expected of us,
and to listen when others shout
though it be painful to hear;
to object, to protest, when we feel, taste, or observe injustice,
believing that even the unjust and arrogant
are human nonetheless
and therefore worthy of strong efforts to reach them.
Take from us, Guiding God, the heart of despair
and fill us with courage and understanding.
Give us a self that knows very well
when the moment has come to protest.
We ask the grace to be angry
when the weakest are the first to be exploited
and the trapped are squeezed for their meager resources,
when the most deserving are the last to thrive,
and the privileged demand more privilege.
We ask for the inspiration to make our voice heard
when we have something that needs to be said,
something that rises to our lips despite our shyness.
And we ask the grace to listen when the meek finally rise to
speak
and their words are an agony for us. . . .

William Cleary, *Psalm Services For Group Prayer*, p. 58

97 *

PART OF OUR LIFE
when good things happen

We thank you, Holy Mystery, She Who Is,
    for all the victories of justice
    that come about, all too seldom, in this world.
It is not sentimentality or wishful thinking
    that make us turn to you in gratitude when such good things
        happen
    for you who long for justice are intimately a part of our life,
    participating in all our anxieties,
    inhabiting all that is,
    yet necessarily leaving humans free and themselves.
Your renewing presence is always and everywhere partial
    to your beloved creatures suffering from socially constructed
        harm,
    to all those working to liberate both oppressed and oppressors
    from the distorted systems that destroy the humanity of them
        both.[105]
We thank you for all progress we have made
    in the attempt to spread shalom throughout the world.
Fill our hearts with your infinite desires
    for true and universal justice.

Sophia, She Who Is, empowering, freeing,
In you we live and move and have our being.

98 *

when praying for wholeness

Creating Wisdom,
    we rejoice in that vision of wholeness
    expressed in the early baptismal hymn:
        we are neither Jew nor Greek,
        neither slave nor free,
        neither male nor female (Gal 3:28)
    for now all are one in a new oneness.[106]
While we work for the coming of the kin-dom of God,
    still there is a longed-for wholeness and healing
    visible in desire even now beneath all differences:
        poor with rich, child with adult, student with teacher,
        well with ill, young with old, enlightened with superstitious,
        male with female, found with lost, living with dead.
While we work to balance and heal differences and injustices,
    be with us in rejoicing in what unites us
    beneath the unfinished work
    of bringing your good order to human affairs.

Caring Mystery, gracing, leading, freeing,
In you we live and move and have our being.

99 ✳

DARK RADIANCE
empowered for public action

Great Mystery of God, Holy Wisdom, She Who Is,
    you are the dark radiance of life
    working in solidarity with the struggle of denigrated persons
    to cast off their mean estate
    and lay hold of their genuine human dignity and value.[107]
When we join in that struggle,
    we feel the warmth of your presence
    and the radiance of your desires.
Inspire us with the energy to participate in building a just global
      society
    along with the humility to submit to the failures
      that mark every such human effort.

Empowering Mystery, loving, helping, freeing,
In you we live and move and have our being.

100 *

EACH SACRAMENT

finding new sacraments

You are our God, Spirit-Sophia, She who is and will always be.
Each sacrament of your presence on earth enlightens us:[108]
    soul-nourishing community,
    mothering heart, fatherly love,
    healing caringness, awesome talent,
    heart-lightening humor, faithful friendship,
    sisterly acceptance, brotherly loyalty,
    astonishing desire.
Our God, your sacramental presence is everywhere,
    through all time, filling all space and distances.
Give us light that we may begin to see evidences of your presence
    everywhere in our world.

Amazing Presence, loving, guiding, freeing,
In you we live and move and have our being.

101 *

NEVER ALONE
when appreciating God's friendship

You, Holy Mystery, are the friend beyond compare.[109]
   In your friendship we can know ourselves
      to be never alone with our personal and globe-encircling
         anxieties,
      but feel supported and energized by your gracious compassion
      and empowering solidarity with us.
Give us enough energy to be useful to our world
   and enough laughter to heal our woundedness
      and illusion-building self-absorption.

Spirit Mystery, guiding, loving, freeing,
In you we live and move and have our being.

102 *

OVERFLOWING WELLSPRING

God as source

Spirit-Sophia, She Who Is,
   you are the freely overflowing wellspring
   of the energy of all creatures who flourish,
   and of the energy of all those
   who resist the diminishment of flourishing,
   both made possible by our participating in your dynamic
      caringness,
   an absolute, relational liveliness that energizes the world.[110]
Be with us, flow into and through us, Holy God!

Creating Mystery, loving, helping, freeing,
In you we live and move and have our being.

103 *

MULTIPLE TRADITIONS
when naming God becomes impossible

Holy Triune Creating Communion,
    Aquinas taught us that we must give you many names[111]
    since language about you
    is always based on your similarity to things we know on earth,
    and creatures are almost endlessly multiple.
The Islamic tradition employs a litany of 99 names
    with the 100th, supposedly your true name, Silence.
Be with us, Creating Silence.
Rabbinic writings provide a rich list of over ninety divine names:
    Friend of the World, Searcher of Hearts,
    Life of the World, The One who understands.
    We thank you for your understanding, your livingness, your
        friendship.
From Africa comes yet another list
    containing a wide variety of names for you:
    Great Mother, Architect of the world,
    Alone the Great One, the One who is everywhere,
    Queen of Heaven, Protector of the Poor.
See how poor we are in our knowledge of you: protect us, Holy
    God.
Our own scripture and inspiration names you in dozens of ways:
The One Who Is—
    which contrasts your perfect existence with our imperfect
        being;
She Who Is—
    which strongly conveys the imaging of yourself
      we find especially in women
    as well as the particular caringness
    which the God of the Burning Bush
      expressed toward the oppressed;
He Who Is—which associates you with the best in male grace;
Spirit-Sophia—a familiar scriptural personification of you
    as maternal, wise, just;

Creator—which places you
   as the Cause of both the material and the spiritual world;
Friend, Lover, Companion—
   which brings out our instinctual reaching out toward you
     imaged forth is all we know of human love;
Ocean, Mountain, Sky,
   suggesting your overwhelming greatness;
Voice, Song, Whisper,
   which stresses your impressive presence
     despite your elusiveness and mystery;
Lord, Spirit-Wind, Father, Mother. . . .
All these multiple efforts to name you or imagine you
   —hovering protective parent bird, a roaring lion, angry mother
     bear—
   give us inklings but ultimately fall short.
Perhaps the cue from Islam is correct:
   it is time again for that reverential abstinence
     from the use of any name for you—
   to indicate how, while incomprehensibly close, you are
     really beyond all naming.
This silence of ours—or the ringing of a bell—
     some substitute for words,
   might better indicate "pointing" than does our use of words,
a naming-toward,
   with all the misleading illusion of understanding
     which words imply.
Give us, Holy God, the patience of searchers
   whose fate may be to never find an answer.

Nameless Mystery, patient, leading, freeing,
In you we live and move and have our being.

· XII ·

. . . an exodus to freedom . . .

The best name for God, according to Aquinas, was supposedly *He who is.* That may even sound comforting and welcome to our ears. It is, however, a male-centered expression, obviously. But it does express the belief that males are made in the image of God. To express the belief that women, too, are made in the image of God (following theologian Elizabeth Johnson), do we not need the expression, at least occasionally, *She Who Is?* Just as male-referent names for God reenforce male-defined values in society, the name She Who Is has wide reenforcing effects on the valuation of women, and with them as symbolic, the valuation of the poor, the marginalized, the meek of the earth, all who suffer oppression and disempowerment. By saying "She Who Is cares infinitely about us all," a new tone of hope for the hopeless is sounded. God is instantly seen as someone on the side of the abused and the weak ones of this world. . . . She Who Is is with us, visits every rape scene, hears the cries of all the poor: something *will* be done about it all! Like the god of the burning bush who felt the oppression of the Hebrew slaves in Egypt, the God of the oppressed certainly plans a path and **an exodus to freedom** for all the poor....

William Cleary, *In God's Presence,* p. 41

104 ✳

IT IS YOU
when wanting to serve

We would be servants of your livingness, Sophia-God, She Who
     Is,
     who gives life to the dead
     and calls into being the things that do not exist (Rom 4:17).
It is you who accompany the lost and defeated
     on the journey to new, unimaginable life.[112]
In you we can hope
     despite anything that disappoints or defeats us.
We put our hope in you,
     that you will bring into being things that do not exist,
     and inspire us with energies
     for justice, earth-care, and community building.

Wisdom, Mystery, loving, leading, freeing,
In you we live and move and have our being.

105 *

ALIVENESS
when prioritizing in prayer

Holy Aliveness, as we "come alive" in stirring moments,
   we find there your special sacrament, your presence.
   In each enthusiasm of our own, we feel your own excitement.
   In moments of wonder we admire your inventiveness.
Holy Aliveness, we give thanks for knowing of you, for knowing
     you.
With your help we shall work against all
   that opposes aliveness and sensitivity, all that is deadening or
     numbing:
   the vulgarization of sexuality, the admiration of violence and
     hurting,
   the commercialization and masculinization of fun and sports,
   and perhaps worst of all,
   the prioritizing of possessions over the human action
     that creates and provides service
     and thus makes real caring and creativity happen.[113]
We would be appreciators of your wonders,
   sympathizers with your resistance
     to whatever degrades our beloved creation,
   and companions and partners to your passion
     for the world's flourishing.[114]

Spirit Aliveness, loving, guiding, freeing,
In you we live and move and have our being.

106 *

SPIRIT WITHIN SOCIETY
when empowered by She Who Is

Holy Mystery,
Incomprehensible Depth of Personal Communion,[115]
    it is your irresistible Wisdom that suggests to us
    that there is everlasting hope for all that is good,
    and limitless strength to resist all that should not be.
We feel empowered when we know
    that you are with us in both our enthusiasms and our
        protests.[116]
Inspire us with authentic selfhood
    and the grace to take ourselves lightly,
    however serious our path
    and seemingly important our inspirations.

Empowering Mystery, loving, helping, freeing,
In you we live and move and have our being.

107 *

SOURCE AND END
returning to God

It is a consolation to us to think, Mother-Sophia,
   Holy Communion of Divine Relationships,
     that you are our journey's end as you were and are its
       beginning.[117]
You are the maternal source of the entire universe,
   its magnificent womb,
     bringing forth at every moment new being,
     new life, new movement and growth, new forms of human
       creativity,
     new levels of wisdom and care
     upon the earth and throughout the cosmos.
If it is wonderful to see a flower emerging shining and fragrant
     from its bud,
   how much more wonderful
   is the emergence of a human child from a mother's womb,
   a world of potency and promise.
But words can't begin to describe the magnificence
   of the entire promise-rich creation
   as it emerges second by second, everywhere at once,
     from your divine womb.
Words fail utterly.
In silence, we observe it.
We turn wordlessly toward you,
   Sophia, Creator Mother, Mystery, Infinite Love, Our God.

Creating Mystery, gifting, loving, freeing,
In you we live and move and have our being.

108 *

INEXHAUSTIBLE SOURCE
turning to She Who Is

Nameless Mystery,
   we give thanks for your presence and strength.
You are sheer, exuberant, relational aliveness
   in the midst of the history of suffering,
   inexhaustible source of new being
   in situations of death and destruction,
   ground of hope for the whole created universe.[118]
Have you patience with our flagging energies,
   our blindness, our small heartedness?
We believe, Holy Mystery. Help thou our unbelief.
   Heal our despair with your sheer aliveness,
      your inexhaustible vitality, and your compassionate joy.

Creating God, empowering and freeing,
In you we live and move and have our being.

109 *

WHAT YOU MEAN TO US
what we think of God

We stretch to describe what you mean to us, Holy Mystery;
   you mother us, as it were,
   you father us perfectly,
   you sister us, you brother us,
   you relate to us in every good way imaginable—and more.
   for you are supremely free and beyond all images.
We can only give thanks to know of you,
   though we cannot really name you or grasp your mystery.[119]

Elusive Mystery, loving, helping, freeing,
In you we live and move and have our being.

110 *

when welcoming otherness

If it is true, Communioning Mystery,
    that mutual relationship of different equals
    appears as the ultimate paradigm of personal and social life,[120]
then give us the graciousness to welcome diversity,
    to celebrate differences, and to cultivate our own uniqueness.
While we pray to become our full and most useful self
    in the work of society and of the planet,
    we ask also for the lightheartedness
    that makes joy a part of all we do.

Sophia, She Who Is, empowering, freeing,
In you we live and move and have our being.

111 ✳

WORD OF LIFE
when facing death

At life's end, you, Mother-Sophia have the last word
  as you had the first, and it is the word of life.
With the same maternal creativity and largess
  by which in the beginning
  you bring into being the things that do not exist,
  you give life to the dead with an outpouring of power
  that radically empowers;[121]
  and your beloved offspring return whence they came,
  mothered through death into life, eternal life.

Creator Mother, giving, taking, freeing,
In you we live and move and have our being.

112 ✳

YOU ARE THE ONE
when resting in Holy Mystery

Holy God,
    though we pursue you avidly in prayer and study,
    we cannot claim to have really understood your Mystery,[122]
    since we know, with Augustine, that
    "if we think we have understood, what we have understood is
        not God."
You are, Holy One, the one who first imagined us,
    dreamed us up, enjoyed the very thought of us—though we
        were not—
    then decided our shape, our visage,
    our abilities and limitations,
    our milieu, our gender, our parents, our siblings,
    our fingerprints, DNA, blood-type, the force of our longings.
You are the One,
    the One Triple Communion of Wisdom, Strength, and Love,
    who parented us far more decisively than did our human
        parents,
    and gave us a role in the life story of the planet.
Like a mother, you, She Who Is, can never forget us,
    or get us out of your thoughts and heart.
Fatherlike too, you, Holy Mystery, hold us in the palm of your
        hand,
    always your newborn, your heir, your child,
    fruit of your lovingness and creative strength.
Our heart rejoices
    to know the embrace of your Parenting Mystery.

Sophia, She Who Is, empowering, freeing,
In you we live and move and have our being.

Book References

Elizabeth A. Johnson, *Consider Jesus*. New York: Crossroad, 1990.

Elizabeth A. Johnson, *She Who Is: The Mystery of God in Feminist Theological Discourse*. New York: Crossroad, 1992.

Elizabeth A. Johnson, *Women, Earth, and Creator Spirit*. New York: Paulist Press, 1993.

William Cleary, *A Doubter's Prayerbook*. New York: Paulist Press, 1994.

William Cleary, *In God's Presence: Centering Experiences for Circles and Solitudes*. Mystic, Conn.: Twenty-Third Publications, 1994.

William Cleary, *Psalm Services For Group Prayer*. Mystic, Conn.: Twenty-Third Publications, 1993.

Endnotes

1. Elizabeth A. Johnson, *She Who Is: The Mystery of God in Feminist Theological Discourse* (New York: Crossroad, 1992), p. 148.
2. Johnson, *She Who Is*, p. 179. In Acts 17:28 Paulis reported using the phrase ("In God we live and move and have our being") with approval when speaking to the Greeks at Athens, ascribing it to "some of your own writers"—as if it were a commonplace expression. The annotations in the Jerusalem Bible ascribe the phrase to Epimenides, a 7th-century BCE Cretan poet and philosopher, so the expression was popular for at least 700 years by the time of Paul.
3. Johnson, *She Who Is*, p. 179.
4. Johnson, *She Who Is*, p. 114.
5. Elizabeth A. Johnson, *Consider Jesus* (New York: Crossroad, 1990), p. 111.
6. Johnson, *She Who Is*, p. 128.
7. Johnson, *She Who Is*, p. 134.
8. Johnson, *She Who Is*, p. 113.
9. Johnson, *She Who Is*, p. 113.
10. Johnson, *She Who Is*, p. 113.
11. Johnson, *She Who Is*, p. 62.
12. Johnson, *She Who Is*, p. 22.
13. Johnson, *She Who Is*, p. 242.
14. Johnson, *She Who Is*, p. 91.
15. Johnson, *She Who Is*, p. 13.
16. Johnson, *She Who Is*, p. 191.
17. Johnson, *She Who Is*, p. 36.
18. Johnson, *She Who Is*, p. 120.
19. Johnson, *She Who Is*, p. 127.
20. Johnson, *She Who Is*, p. 109.
21. Johnson, *She Who Is*, p. 110.
22. Johnson, *She Who Is*, p. 139.
23. Johnson, *She Who Is*, p. 91.
24. Johnson, *She Who Is*, p. 266.
25. Johnson, *She Who Is*, p. 239.

26. Johnson, *She Who Is*, p. 240.
27. Johnson, *She Who Is*, p. 229.
28. Johnson, *She Who Is*, p. 229.
29. Johnson, *She Who Is*, p. 243.
30. Johnson, *She Who Is*, p. 256.
31. Johnson, *She Who Is*, p. 65.
32. Johnson, *She Who Is*, p. 65.
33. Johnson, *She Who Is*, p. 146.
34. Johnson, *She Who Is*, p. 170.
35. Johnson, *She Who Is*, p. 231.
36. Johnson, *She Who Is*, p. 232.
37. Johnson, *She Who Is*, p. 231.
38. Johnson, *She Who Is*, p. 228.
39. Johnson, *She Who Is*, p. 240.
40. Johnson, *She Who Is*, p. 133.
41. Johnson, *She Who Is*, p. 135.
42. Johnson, *She Who Is*, p. 91.
43. Johnson, *She Who Is*, p. 83.
44. Johnson, *She Who Is*, p. 128.
45. Johnson, *She Who Is*, p. 140.
46. Johnson, *She Who Is*, p. 150.
47. Johnson, *She Who Is*, p. 169.
48. Johnson, *She Who Is*, p. 163.
49. Johnson, *She Who Is*, p. 267.
50. Johnson, *She Who Is*, p. 159.
51. Johnson, *She Who Is*, p. 165.
52. Johnson, *She Who Is*, p. 257.
53. Johnson, *She Who Is*, p. 175.
54. Johnson, *She Who Is*, p. 233.
55. Johnson, *She Who Is*, p. 223.
56. Johnson, *She Who Is*, p. 180.
57. Johnson, *She Who Is*, p. 184.
58. Johnson, *She Who Is*, p. 191.
59. Johnson, *She Who Is*, p. 101.
60. Johnson, *She Who Is*, p. 179.
61. Johnson, *She Who Is*, p. 185.
62. Johnson, *She Who Is*, p. 229.
63. Johnson, *She Who Is*, p. 146.
64. Johnson, *She Who Is*, p. 170.
65. Johnson, *She Who Is*, p. 181.
66. Johnson, *She Who Is*, p. 229.
67. Johnson, *She Who Is*, p. 243.
68. Johnson, *She Who Is*, p. 5.
69. Johnson, *She Who Is*, p. 245.
70. Johnson, *She Who Is*, p. 265.
71. Johnson, *She Who Is*, p. 83.

72. Johnson, *She Who Is*, p. 149, 123.
73. Johnson, *She Who Is*, p. 157.
74. Johnson, *She Who Is*, p. 243.
75. Johnson, *She Who Is*, p. 229.
76. Johnson, *She Who Is*, p. 227.
77. Johnson, *She Who Is*, p. 251.
78. Johnson, *She Who Is*, p. 215.
79. Johnson, *She Who Is*, p. 205.
80. Johnson, *She Who Is*, p. 192.
81. Johnson, *She Who Is*, p. 110.
82. Johnson, *She Who Is*, p. 228.
83. Johnson, *She Who Is*, p. 216.
84. Johnson, *She Who Is*, p. 213.
85. Johnson, *She Who Is*, p. 247.
86. Johnson, *She Who Is*, p. 270.
87. Johnson, *She Who Is*, p. 246.
88. Johnson, *She Who Is*, p. 260.
89. Johnson, *She Who Is*, p. 261.
90. Johnson, *She Who Is*, p. 264.
91. Johnson, *She Who Is*, p. 101.
92. Johnson, *She Who Is*, p. 65.
93. Johnson, *She Who Is*, p. 270.
94. Johnson, *She Who Is*, p. 138.
95. Johnson, *She Who Is*, p. 222.
96. *She Who Is*, videotape, Earth Communications, Laurel, Md.
97. Psalm 136:8.
98. Johnson, *She Who Is*, p. 62.
99. Johnson, *She Who Is*, p. 230.
100. Johnson, *She Who Is*, p. 229.
101. Johnson, *She Who Is*, p. 241.
102. Johnson, *She Who Is*, p. 105.
103. Johnson, *She Who Is*, p. 258.
104. Johnson, *She Who Is*, p. 260.
105. Johnson, *She Who Is*, p. 136.
106. Johnson, *She Who Is*, p. 31.
107. Johnson, *She Who Is*, p. 244.
108. Johnson, *She Who Is*, p. 124.
109. Johnson, *She Who Is*, p. 145.
110. Johnson, *She Who Is*, p. 243.
111. Johnson, *She Who Is*, p. 117.
112. Johnson, *She Who Is*, p. 244.
113. Johnson, *She Who Is*, p. 252.
114. Johnson, *She Who Is*, p. 244.
115. Johnson, *She Who Is*, p. 228.
116. Johnson, *She Who Is*, p. 159.
117. Johnson, *She Who Is*, p. 181.

118. Johnson, *She Who Is,* p. 243.
119. Johnson, *She Who Is,* p. 175.
120. Johnson, *She Who Is,* p. 222.
121. Johnson, *She Who Is,* p. 181.
122. Johnson, *She Who Is,* p. 105.

I AM WHO AM

Jean Morningstar, osym '94

Also from Crossroad

ELIZABETH A. JOHNSON
She Who Is
The Mystery of God in
Feminist Theological Discourse

"The most substantial and sophisticated effort yet undertaken to connect 'feminist and classical wisdom' in a synthesis at once engaged with the classical sources of Christian theology and committed to a vision of Christianity pervasively and profoundly marked by feminist values. . . . And she has performed the most fundamental function of a true theologian, which is to provide a vision of God worthy of prayer."

—*Commonweal*

0-8245-1162-X hc $24.95
0-8245-1376-2 pb $16.95

ELIZABETH A. JOHNSON
Consider Jesus
Waves of Renewal in Christology

"Thoughtful readers will find profound theological insights into the person and mission of Jesus Christ in Consider Jesus. . . . To read Consider Jesus is to experience popular theology at its very best."

—*Sisters Today*

0-8245-1161-1 pb $10.95

Please ask for these books at your bookstore, or to order directly, send payment (including $3.00 for shipping and handling, plus $1.00 for each additional book) to The Crossroad Publishing Company, 370 Lexington Avenue, New York, NY 10017.